Memoir
AND WRITINGS OF
Jacob M. Pike

Memoir
and writings of
Jacob M. Pike

Transcribed, Edited, and Annotated by

PETER PIKE JR.

Introduction, Endnotes, and Maps. Copyright © 2020 by Peter Pike Jr.

All rights reserved, including the right to reproduce this book or portions thereof in any form whatsoever, except for brief quotations in articles and reviews

Book design by Kathryn E. Campbell

ISBN: 978-1-7321645-3-6

To the descendants of

Jacob M. Pike (1831-1916)

and

Mary L. Howell (1842-1892)

CONTENTS

Introduction ix

Memoir of Jacob M. Pike 1

    Addendum 41

    Endnotes 45

Other Writings

    Chased by a Bear, 1850 69

    Shooting a Grizzly Bear, 1853 71

    Mining with the Hatheway Brothers, 1854 73

    Trip to Yosemite Valley in the Spring of 1857 77

    Drumming Trip to Washington Territory, 1878 83

Appendix—Shootout on the Stanislaus River

    San Joaquin Republican (Stockton), Aug. 7, 1858 89

    Daily Alta California (San Francisco), Aug. 8, 1858 91

    Sacramento Daily Union, Aug. 19, 1858 93

Photographs

    Jacob Pike and Drummers, 1866 27

    Jacob Pike, 1876 30

    Mary Pike, 1878 31

    Jacob Pike, 1903 36

Maps

    Gold Country–Jacob Pike, 1850–1865 9

    Howell Farm and Central Ferry Road, 1859 21

    Tuolumne River Bars 43

Credits 97

About the Editor 99

INTRODUCTION

JACOB PIKE'S MEMOIR holds a sacred place in family lore. Handwritten in 1912, sixty-two years after he jumped ship in San Francisco at age eighteen, Jacob's manuscript describes his colorful life in the Golden State. Four years after writing his memoir, Jacob died in San Francisco at age eighty-four in 1916.

Although he never struck it rich, he always worked tirelessly to succeed—as a gold miner, storekeeper, restaurateur, and many other occupations. Like most Californians, his life was filled with both success and failure. As he wrote, financial setbacks always gave him "more energy."

Sometimes Jacob did not place his recollections in chronological order, and sometimes he did not remember the correct date of an event. This explains why his narrative, especially during his early years in California, jumps back and forth in time. Even so, the historical characters and actions documented in my endnotes do correspond to his amazing recall of events.

To improve readability, I have corrected minor grammatical and factual errors, and I have added section headings to break up the largely paragraphless manuscript. Otherwise, his memoir reads word-for-word as he wrote it. The original sixty-three-page manuscript rests today in the Bancroft Library at the University of California, Berkeley.

Peter Pike Jr.

MEMOIR OF JACOB M. PIKE

A BOY'S LIFE IN MAINE*

Was born in Eastport, State of Maine, August 23, 1831.¹ My father was drowned at sea. He was then 33 years old.² Were five children of us, four boys and one girl.³ Our sister was born a short time after her father's death. I was five years at the time of Father's death. We lived with Grandfather and Grandmother. We were poor, and, a short time after Father's death, my Mother went out Nursing. Followed that profession for several years.

Samuel and George, the two oldest brothers, were bound out to learn a trade. William and I were going to school. At fourteen years of age I was anxious to go to sea. Mother was having a hard time getting along, and I wanted to assist her all I could. She said I was too young and would not consent for me to leave home, but I kept continually teasing her to go to sea.

Finally, she went to my Guardian, Mr. Houghton⁴ of Eastport and asked his advice. He told her that she had better let me go for, after I took one voyage, that would cure me of going to sea. There was a new bark⁵ in Eastport ready for sea under Captain Dunham,⁶ and Mother went to see him and ask him to take me as Cabin boy. He said he would.

---

* Section headings added to handwritten manuscript.

So the next morning I went to the school house and got my book and that day went aboard the bark and sailed the next day for Barbados, one of the islands in the West Indies. We were loaded with lumber for that port. From there we went to another island called Turks Island [in the Bahamas] and took on a load of salt for New York. From there went to Eastport for another load of lumber.

Crew was paid off in Eastport. We had two months' pay due us. My wage was six dollars a month. I drew four dollars while I was on the voyage and had eight dollars coming to me. Was paid off in fifty-cent pieces, sixteen pieces. I thought it a pile of money. I put it all in my handkerchief and carried it home to Mother and emptied it on her lap. I said, "There, Mother, there is eight dollars for you." She said, "My son, I can buy my winter's wood with that money." That was late in the fall.

I remained in that bark three years in the West Indies trade and helped my Mother all the time. Then I joined a brig[7] and took a load of passengers for Chagres[8] to go to California via Panama. That was 1848. We lay in the mouth of the Chagres River for three weeks waiting for orders. We finally received them to go to San Juan for a load of Indigo & hides [and] from there to go to New York. Before I left the Chagres River, I was taken sick with Chagres fever[9] and was sick all the way to New York and, after arriving there, I went to the hospital. Was there three weeks before I was well. Then I went home. Stayed some little time.

I forgot to mention that as soon as I started to sea, I commenced to learn navigation. Captain Dunham, knowing my Mother, took an interest in me and, when I left the ship, I could navigate a ship as good as anybody.

GOLD RUSH BOUND
1849, Age 18

A New York ship came to Eastport called *Nathaniel Hooper*[10] loaded with lumber. She shipped most of her crew in Eastport. I made application for a position as Able Seaman and was accepted. We all signed articles to go to San Francisco to unload there and then to go to China from there and back to New York. The voyage was not to exceed two years. We had five passengers for San Francisco. I was then eighteen years old.[11]

She had shipped all hands necessary with the exception of the Second Mate. It seemed the Captain had been told I knew navigation and was a good sailor. The Captain called me aft and asked me to take the position as Second Mate of the ship. I told him I was pretty young to accept that position. He said he had been told I was fully capable of filling that position and wanted me to fill it. I said all right, I would do the best I could.

He called all the sailors aft and told them he had appointed Mr. Pike Second Mate of the ship and instructed them to recognize me as Second Mate of the ship. So I took my baggage out of the forecastle and moved into the cabin and messed [ate] with the Captain and Mate.[12]

MUTINY AT SEA

We sailed from Eastport on July 10th, 1849. Everything went along all right for a while. But the Mate was proving himself to be a brute.[13] One day he sent a sailor up to the main-topmast to do something. It seemed he did not understand his order fully and made some little mistake. The Mate took a rope's end and went up to the main-topmast and gave the sailor a hard whipping. That started an ill will toward the Mate by the sailors, and Hell was a popping between the Mate and the crew until later on.

A few days after that we crossed the Gulf Stream. A sailor came to me (he knew I was keeping position of the ship every day) and asked me to let him know when we were in the latitude of Rio de Janeiro. I asked him what for. He said nothing in particular. But I smelled a rat.

However, the Mate was such a brute that, when we got to the latitude of Rio de Janeiro, I told him. Then things commenced popping. The crew rose up and placed both Captain and Mate prisoners in the forecastle and requested me to take the ship into Rio de Janeiro. I changed the course of the ship for that port.

However, the passengers, I thought, ought to be consulted. So I called them together. They said they would go and see the Captain and see if he would not run the ship into Rio de Janeiro. I told the crew to let the passengers go and see the Mate & Captain. They did so. The Captain agreed to run the ship into St. Catherine's,[14] a port sixty miles south of Rio de Janeiro.

I advised the crew to let the Captain & Mate take charge of the ship, and I would inform them if the Captain put the ship on the right course. They released the Captain & Mate, and the ship was put on the right course. We arrived three days after we shaped our course for St. Catherine's.

Soon as we dropped anchor in the harbor, the Captain hoisted a signal for the American Consul.[15] He came aboard the ship with some Negro soldiers and took the crew ashore and placed them in prison on a charge of mutiny. They did not have any trial. Kept them in prison three weeks and discharged them.

It was hard to ship a crew there. Had to wait there four weeks before we could get a crew. Finally, we got the number of men we wanted and sailed for San Francisco. We arrived off Cape Horn, within sight of the Cape. Before we got around, we took a SW gale[16] of wind and drove us to latitude 60° south in freezing weather. Finally, the gale abated, and we commenced to put on sail.

MIRACULOUS FALL OFF A YARDARM

We were running under single-reefed topsails. We had a Liverpool boy as one of the sailors. I ordered him to go aloft and loosen the main topgallant sail and set it over the single-reefed main topsail. It was cold, and I told him the rigging and yards were full of ice, and, if he went aloft with those heavy boots on, he would be apt to fall. He said he would run the risk. So he went up to the main topgallant yard and loosened the sail.

When that was done, I told him to go down on the main topsail yard and pull the foot of the topgallant sail to windward over the main topmast stay so that the men could sheet it home. Just as he stepped on the yard, his foot slipped and down he came, a distance of 70 feet. In falling, he struck the fore brace and from there he struck the belly of the mainsail and from there to the deck. I, of course, thought he was dead.

I carried him to the cabin and commenced rubbing him with spirits. He came to in about 15 minutes. With the exception of a badly bruised shoulder and head, there was not a broken bone in his body. Striking the belly of the mainsail broke the force of the fall. It was the luckiest escape from death I ever saw or ever heard of. He was able to go on his duties in two weeks. From there, there was nothing worth mentioning until arriving in San Francisco.

After leaving St. Catherine's, the Mate behaved himself better. He thought it did not pay to beat and bang men as he did at the commencement of the voyage. On February 4, 1850,[17] we took on a pilot and sailed into the harbor of San Francisco and dropped anchor, just eight months from Eastport.

BROTHER SAM SURPRISES JACOB
1850, Age 19

When I left Eastport, I left my brother Sam home. At that time, he was not thinking of coming to San Francisco. As I said before, I signed ship's articles for the round-the-world voyage, not to exceed two years from Eastport to San Francisco, from there to China and then to New York.

I had already made up my mind to run away from the ship and stay in the land of gold. You can imagine my surprise when the first man that came over the ship's rail was my brother Sam.[18] He surely was a welcome angel. Before he left the ship, we had made arrangements for him to hire a boat and come under the ship's bow that night and take me and baggage ashore. He came to the ship as per appointment and away we went ashore—once more a free man.[19]

We went to the State of Maine Hotel.[20] San Francisco was a very small place, one small wharf and a few houses. The State of Maine Hotel was, I think, the best in town and did not have a bedstead in it. It had bunks built like they are for sailors in a forecastle in a ship. Sam was working at his trade at good wages and next thing for me to do was to get some work.

I went down to the wharf and saw a ship laying there dismasted. She had a rigger aboard. I found out who was the boss and asked if he wanted any more men. He asked me if I was a sailor and understood this kind of work. I told him I understood it thoroughly. He told me to go to work. You bet I did for I did not have a cent. Left all of my pay when I ran away [from my ship].

On this job, I got 5.00 dollars a day, so I felt like a heavy bond holder. I worked on the job until we finished and hauled the ship out in the stream. Her name was the *Raven*[21] of Boston, and when we got through, she was as pretty as pink. The Captain of her wanted and tried every means to have me ship with him as Second Mate. But I declined. I was in California, and in California I was going to stay.

SEARCHING FOR GOLD

Sam proposed to go to the Southern Mines.[22] I said all right. So we took passage on a little steamer for San Joaquin City.[23] It was called a city, but I think there was one store, a blacksmith shop, and saloon. That constituted a city in those days. It was right at the mouth of the Stanislaus River[24] that emptied into the San Joaquin River.

The point we were making for was Spark's Ferry[25] on the Tuolumne River, a small mining camp. From where we walked, it was fifty miles and no transportation. So Sam and I started afoot to make it, packing our blankets on our backs. We arrived there in a little less than three days, pretty well used up boys. I had blisters on my feet three inches long.

Spark's Ferry was a very poor mining town at the time. In later years it turned out to be a good one with improved machinery. From there we went up to Roger's Bar[26] about six miles up the river. When we arrived there, the people were making up a company to turn the river, and Sam and I joined the company. There were fifty members. They were principally from Maine and Nantucket. Most of us were sailors. This was about the 15th of May [1850].

We had a big job ahead of us—a dam across the river to build out of logs and two-inch planks and digging a canal through the bar of solid rock or nearly so, about four-hundred feet long. It was a great mistake on the part of Sam and I to have joined the company. For had we worked a rocker washing the surface dirt from the bar, we would have made good money all summer. As it was, by the time we got our dam built and tunnel dug to carry the water, the fall rains came very early and flooded us out. And all our summer's work was lost.[27]

MORE BAD LUCK

Then four of us went to Big Oak Flat[28] for winter diggings, built a log house and laid in our winter's grub. At that place, you could not work without rain. We got all comfortably settled in our new log cabin and ready to work if the rain came. It was in the rainy season and, of course, we expected it to rain. But to our disgust and surprise, none came. Never mined a day all winter. It was the record-breaking dry winter.

Soon as spring opened, Sam & I went down to Stevens' Bar[29] on the Tuolumne River and went to work. We worked as long as it would pay, I think about two weeks. And we heard of better diggings down at Morgan's Bar.[30] So we packed up and started down river. Night overtook us and we stopped at Hawkins' Bar[31] and asked the storekeeper if he would allow us to sleep on the store floor. He said yes. So we spread our blankets on the store floor and turned in to our soft bed.

The money we made at Steven's Bar I had in a buckskin purse in my pants pocket. There was one hundred and twenty dollars in it in gold dust. When we got up in the morning, we could not find my money. It had worked out of my pants during the night. Someone picked it up on the floor. That left us without a cent.

We started with our blankets on our backs for Morgan's Bar. We arrived there before dark. We had heard previous to this that a man from Maine kept a store at Morgan's Bar. Soon as we struck camp, we went to see Mr. Nelson. We told him we were from Maine and told him our hard luck story about losing all our money at Hawkins' Bar the night before and that we were dead broke and wanted to know if he would give us credit for some grub and cooking utensils. We wanted to go to work on the bar.

He says, "You look like pretty nice boys. 'By James Priestly Moses,' you can have anything I have got in the store." That sounded pretty good about that time. He put up a fine outfit for us, and he gave us the privilege to sleep

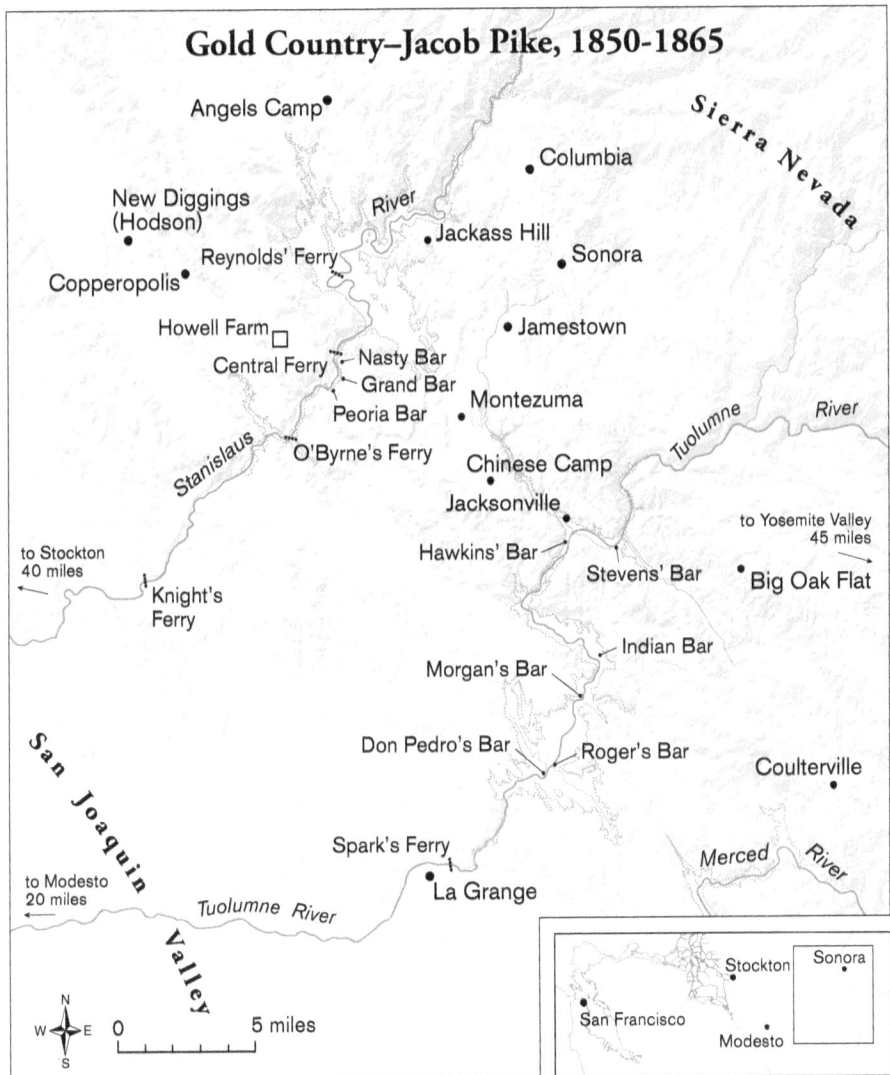

Note: On this relief map, gray lines show the historic river courses, and dotted lines show modern reservoirs. Along the Stanislaus River, Tulloch Lake now covers Peoria Bar, Grand Bar, Nasty Bar, O'Byrne's Ferry, and the Central Ferry, and New Melones Lake covers Reynolds' Ferry. Along the Tuolumne River, Lake Don Pedro now covers Don Pedro's Bar, Roger's Bar, Morgan's Bar, Indian Bar, Hawkins' Bar, and Stevens' Bar.

on the floor in the store. That was fine.

Next morning, we got some lumber from Mr. Nelson to build a cradle, and Sam went to work and built a fine cradle,[32] he being a carpenter. It came in mighty handy. We went out and located a claim on the bar from the water up to the top of [the] bar. Sam rocked the cradle, and I dug and packed the dirt to him in two buckets. It paid fine. I think we made sixteen dollars that day. We were as happy as could be.

In a few days, we made enough to pay our store bill. You bet our credit was established. You bet I never put any more gold dust in my pocket again. We worked there three or four weeks and made quite a little stake. We had worked up to the top of the bar and the pay ran down to four or five dollars per day each. Sam said he would not work for so small pay. I told him I thought we had better keep on. He said no, we would hunt for better diggings.

So we left our claim and went down to Don Pedro's Bar.[33] A few days after we left our claim at Morgan's Bar, two men went into the hole we left and on the top of the bar struck rich dirt. They had struck an old river channel running through there, and, in a short space of time, they worked into the rich channel and in about three months they took out seventy thousand dollars. That surely was too bad. If we had worked our claim a few days longer, if we had done so, all that gold dust would have been our own.

We did not do much after we went to Don Pedro's Bar, and I became disgusted because we had bad luck for nearly a year and had not made more than a living. I told Sam I would go to San Francisco and go to sea again. Before I started for the mines, I packed my sextant, logbooks, and all of my navigation books in a box and stored them in a storehouse. In the early part of 1851, the storehouse burnt up with all its contents.[34] That was a great loss to me, for I would have enjoyed them much to refer to now. That was more of my bad luck.

BACK TO THE SEA

1851, Age 20

Well, I went to San Francisco. The first day I was there, I was walking along Front Street, and who should I meet? It was Charlie Hatheway. I said, "Charlie where the devil did you come from?" He said, "I came from Honolulu. I came there in a New York ship and ran away from her there and came here on a steamer." He asked me how long I had been in California. I told him about a year, and I had just come from the mines perfectly disgusted with them. And had come down to ship out and go to sea and he had better come with me. He said, "All right."

I forgot to mention that he and I went to school together in Eastport. Next day we shipped on board a square-rigged brig bound for San Pedro [Los Angeles] and Acapulco, Mexico. We sailed the following day and arrived in San Pedro, where we discharged our cargo. Then we sailed for Acapulco, Mexico. We arrived in due time, discharged our cargo, and the brig was sold to the Mexican government. We were paid off and went ashore.

In the meantime, Charlie was taken sick with a fever. We were in a foreign port, and the American Consul had to look out for American sailors. Now the question arose, how we were going to get back to San Francisco? Charlie was convalescing but was not strong enough to leave.

The American sloop of war, *Vincennes*, came into port.[35] I heard she was shorthanded. So I watched for the Captain to come ashore. Finally, he came. I took off my hat to him and told him I heard he was shorthanded. He said he was. I told him I was a sailor and wanted to go to San Francisco. Also, I told him I had come here in a vessel from San Francisco, and she was sold to the Mexican government. That was the reason I was stranded here. The Captain said, "All right young man, you can ship for San Francisco."

So I went to Charlie and told him I could go up to San Francisco in the sloop of war *Vincennes*. I had seen the American Consul and told him soon as Charlie was able to leave to get him a chance to go to San Francisco. So I went aboard the sloop of war. We had a fine passage up of three weeks. The Captain wanted me to stay by the ship. I told him I could not, that I preferred to stay in California. So I was paid off and went ashore.

SEARCHING FOR GOLD, AGAIN

A short time after I had left brother Sam, he received a letter from Eastport that his wife had died, and he immediately went home to settle some business he had there with a view of returning to California as soon as that was accomplished. I made up my mind not to leave San Francisco until he arrived here. In the meantime, I wrote him that I would stay in San Francisco until he returned here.

It was not very long before I received a letter from him saying he would arrive in San Francisco at a certain date with our youngest brother, William. They arrived in April (I have forgotten the date) 1852. After a few days we started for the mines and brought up on the Tuolumne River at Morgan's Bar, the same place we had left a year before.

One Sunday I was walking up the river. I saw a man coming down the river. As I came near to him, I says to myself, if that ain't Charlie Hatheway,[36] it is his ghost, and sure enough it was he. I asked him, "How the devil did you get here?" He said he came from Acapulco on a steamer to San Francisco and was mining Indian Bar[37] just above Morgan's Bar. We mined a good deal since and have been in touch with each other ever since, up to the present date [1912]. We worked for some time on the river but did not make more than a living.

ALMOST BURIED ALIVE

1854, Age 23

There is one more instance of my narrow escapes that I forgot to mention, before I went to the Stanislaus River in 1854. On my way to the Stanislaus River, I stopped overnight at Montezuma.[38] I met an old friend there by the name of Day. He told me that he had a claim there, and, if I wished, I could go in partners with him and work.

He said we would have to run a tunnel in the hill and strike the pay gravel which would be about fifty feet. It was said to be good rich pay gravel. So I told Mr. Day I would go in with him. The next day we started in to run a cut in the hill preparatory to starting the tunnel. We finally started the tunnel. We were drifting in hard cement ground, and the cement was full of seams or cracks.

When we got in about ten feet, a large cement boulder weighing at least 500 lbs. fell from the side of the drift and struck me a glancing blow on my left hip, just scratching the skin off my hip. I told Mr. Day we had better get out, that some more cement boulders may fall, and we would not get off so easy as we have with this one that just fell.

We picked our tools up and came out. We had not been out over five minutes when our tunnel and the front of the cut caved in with a roaring noise. Had we not left where we were working, it would have taken a crew of men a week to have dug out our bodies. That is what I call a narrow escape from death. This Montezuma story occurred in 1854 and ought to go in my memoirs after leaving Coulterville[39] and going to the Stanislaus River.

SAM BUILDS A MINING MACHINE

We heard of good diggings over on the Stanislaus River, and we all picked up and went over there. We located claims on Grand Bar[40] and Nasty Bar.[41] Charlie Hatheway was with us. Sam being a carpenter, we concluded to improve on the slow style of cradle mining. So Sam made out a bill of lumber for two wheels to raise the water fifteen feet.

We soon got our lumber and went to work, Sam bossing. We built two boats, scow fashion. Dimensions about thirty feet long and five feet wide, square at both ends. The boats were tied strongly together with scantling 4x6, boats five feet apart, the wheel that runs between the boats, the paddles are 4-1/2 feet long, and wheel thirty feet in diameter, hung on a shaft in the center, hoist and lower with a tackle on each end of the shaft.

There are wooden buckets on each of the paddles 6x10. As the wheel turns, the buckets empty their water in a receiver and the water runs in sluices to the sluice boxes that wash out the gold. The boats are placed right at the head of a riffle in the river. The strong current turns the wheel.

That scheme was a great revolution in mining in those days. You could handle so much more dirt by raising your water with a wheel than you could with a cradle, thereby making much more money. When we got our wheels in operation, we had fine diggings and made some money. Everybody that could had wheels on boats after we started ours.

GUNFIRE IN JACOB'S STORE
1857, Age 26

After I had mined awhile, I bought out Fred Lux's[42] store at Peoria Bar,[43] just below Grand Bar. This location was a hard place for rough characters. The first fight I had in my store was between Tom Reynolds and Gen. Harrison. They had been playing cards and got to quarreling. I finally got them separated and got Gen. Harrison to go to bed. I let Tom Reynolds sleep in the store that night.

Next morning about six o'clock, Tom was getting up. All at once, I see the door open suddenly, and there was General Harrison with six-shooter in hand, taking aim at Tom, who was getting up and had just buckled on his six-shooter. As I said, I see Harrison at the door with six-shooter in hand. I was about fifteen feet from him. I made a rush for him and, before I could disarm him, he had shot Tom twice, once through his mouth, took four of his teeth out, & once through the fleshy part of his right arm. His mouth was bleeding, so I thought he was killed.

By this time, others came into the store, and we picked Tom up and washed him off and found the ball went through his mouth. The only harm done he was minus four teeth, and the ball that went through his arm did not break any bones. So it was a close call. He got well quick. This man, Gen'l Harrison, was one of the most desperate men on the river, and he had killed several men. Always had a six-shooter and a tomahawk on his belt. But he soon got his desserts.

He left Peoria Bar and went down river a short distance just after he shot Tom Reynolds. He got in a quarrel with a miner. They were separated. That same night he (Harrison) was shot dead in his bed in a tent in which he lived. No one knew who shot him, but it was supposed it was the man that he had quarreled with.

There was no effort to find out. Of course, it was a cowardly act. But he was such a dangerous man, everybody was glad to hear of his death. I know I was for he had threatened to kill me for twisting the six-shooter out of his hand when he shot Tom Reynolds. So after he was killed, my mind was at ease that he was dead.

BATTLE ON THE STANISLAUS RIVER

1858, Age 27

Next shooting scrape we had was between two mining companies.[44] One had a claim on Grand Bar.[45] The other was two Frenchmen who had a claim just below them. They built a dam across the river to turn the water out of the river so they could mine the riverbed. The claim above had a water wheel, the same as I explained to you before. They were the oldest company and, according to the mining laws on the river, had the prior right.

When the Frenchmen got their dam finished, it backed the water up on the wheel above so it would not turn, stopping the [original] company from working their mine. They went to the Frenchmen and told them they were the oldest company. Consequently, they had the prior right, and they [the Frenchmen] had no right to back the water up on them and stop their work. And if they did not stop backing the water up on them, they would pull their dam down. The next day the Frenchmen made no effort to remedy the trouble.

I expected there would be trouble. A man by the name of Jim Oliphant and I were in my store. All at once I heard the report of gunshots. I told Jim those fellows up there are in trouble. We buckled on our six-shooters and ran up and found the company above had come down to tear the dam down.

The Frenchmen were in their tent near the dam and opened fire on the three men that were tearing down the dam. One was killed, one mortally wounded; he died in a few days after. The other had seven large buckshot in his legs. He got well. It surely looked like a battlefield. The two Frenchmen in the meantime had crossed the river and went up a steep hill.

By that time there was quite a crowd gathered. Twelve of us formed a posse and went after the Frenchmen. We followed them to the top of the hill and then concluded to divide our party and take different directions. A man by the name of Geo. Warren[46] headed one party and followed up the river. I headed the other party and followed along the valley, enquiring at every house we came to if the two Frenchmen had been seen. Could not get any information.

So we concluded to come back to Lawhead's Ferry,[47] which is just above where the shooting took place. While resting there, we heard the report of guns and in a few minutes two of Geo. Warren's party came running down the trail all covered with blood and reported they met the Frenchmen about a quarter of a mile above and they [the Frenchmen] had shot them. One was shot through the breast. Ball went through his breast between the breastbone and flesh. The other was shot in the head, and it was only a scalp wound. Both got well very quick.

All of Geo. Warren's party had come in excepting Geo. Warren. "My god," said I. "Is it possible they have killed George?" So several of us went up the trail to investigate. We soon found his body being right near a big boulder. He was the head man coming along the trail. The Frenchmen and our boys met almost face to face. The Frenchmen were as quick as lightning with a shotgun and got in the first shot, and poor George Warren fell dead with a whole charge of buckshot in his breast. He was a splendid fellow and was an awful thing that his life should be sacrificed in such a way.

The Frenchmen went to Sonora and were secreted by their countrymen and very soon took passage for their own country. That is so I was told. That surely was a day of slaughter, 3 killed and three wounded. It was a lucky thing that I did not go as leader with George Warren's men. If I had, I would have been served the same as he.

QUARREL LEADS TO DOUBLE MURDER*

A short time after that, it was July 4, 1857,[48] two miners got to quarrelling in my store. I got them outside. As soon as I did one of them drew his six-shooter. The other drew his knife and both commenced. One shot. The other cut. They both fell dead in their tracks. It was the most desperate fight that ever occurred in my neighborhood. I was getting tired of taking so many chances with my life, so I concluded to sell my store. I finally sold it to James Oliphant.[49]

JACOB'S SAWMILL VENTURE FAILS*
1856, Age 25

Brother Sam, who was living in Montezuma, told me that Uriah Nelson[50] was trying to get up a company to buy a ranch and sawmill near Coulterville, Mariposa County.[51] So I, with Nelson and two others, bought the property. That was in 1856. It was a fine piece of property. But we could not agree on the management of it. So I sold out. A little while before I sold, I will tell you of a little hanging scrape we had.

TYING A HANGMAN'S KNOT*

There were general complaints about people robbing and killing Chinamen around Coulterville. A great many Chinamen were mining near Coulterville. Coulterville received a big trade from the Chinamen, and there is where the complaints were coming from. So we organized a Committee [52] to investigate and stop this robbing and killing if we possibly could.

---

* Incidents not in chronological order, but as written by Jacob.

We went to work, and in a week we had two Mexicans arrested. In the meantime, we secured ample evidence of their guilt. We had them tried. One was convicted of murder in the first degree. The other was discharged with a promise that he would leave town immediately. You ought to have seen that fellow skip out of town.

After he got out, the sentence of the other one was to be hung immediately. This work was all done by our committee, not by a Court of Justice. That is the way we used to do it in those days. Courts were too slow, and so seldom were convictions procured. Well, the hanging had to take place.

We rustled up a horse and cart and placed a board across the body of the cart. We placed the prisoner on the board with his hands tied behind him and drove him to an oak tree that we had selected. We drove up under a limb and threw the rope we had procured over the limb. The next question was, Who could tie a hangman's knot? The crowd was canvassed, and no one could tie a hangman's knot. I did not let anyone know I could tie one.

Finally, I said I could tie one. So I took the end of the rope and tied one, all hands looking on to see me do it, and placed the rope properly around the fellow's neck. The rope was pulled tight and made fast. When that was done, the prisoner, who was sitting back to the driver, turned his head around to the driver and said *pronto*, that in Spanish means to go ahead quick. So the driver drove out from under him and let him swing out from the cart. The rope was so nicely adjusted around his neck, he died in ten minutes. His friends took the body down and buried it.

Mr. Cashman, a storekeeper in the town, furnished the rope.[53] We gave it out that the Committee would continue to be under organization and, if necessary, Mr. Cashman would furnish the rope and Mr. Pike would tie the knot to hang anyone that was found guilty of murder. The stand we took in this matter was the cause of all bad characters leaving Coulterville and the surrounding neighborhood. And from that day to this [1912], there has not been any trouble in Coulterville of any serious nature. This occurred in 1857.

JACOB OPENS NEW STORE
1858, Age 27

After I settled my business at the mill, I went to Salt Spring Valley in Calaveras County.[54] Built a store and started business in 1858.[55] My customers were farmers & miners. I had a two-horse delivery wagon and used to go down to the Stanislaus River with a load of goods about every week, which was about six miles.[56]

There was a family by the name of Howell, who lived about five miles from my store.[57] Mr. Howell's house was right on the side of the road that I drove to the river to deliver my goods. I had heard of his fine-looking daughter, and later I saw her several times.[58] But I did not get an introduction. I had made up my mind that all the reports I had heard of her were true. I thought if I could get an introduction, I would be all right.

HIS HORSE BALKS, HE MEETS MARY
1859, Ages–Jacob 28, Mary 17

One day I had occasion to go to the river with a load of goods, which I delivered. In coming home, I had to drive up a very steep hill.[59] Right at the top of the hill, my near horse balked and would not move an inch. After a long time trying to make him go, he lay over the top of the wagon tongue and broke about three feet off the end of it. That made me red hot mad. I took the end of the tongue and hit him between the eyes. The iron that keeps the yoke from pulling back on the tongue went square into his brain, and the blow killed the horse.

The next question was, Where was I going to get a horse to work it home? The idea popped into my head in a moment to go to Mr. Howell's place about a mile away and borrow a horse. Off I started thinking all the time I might get

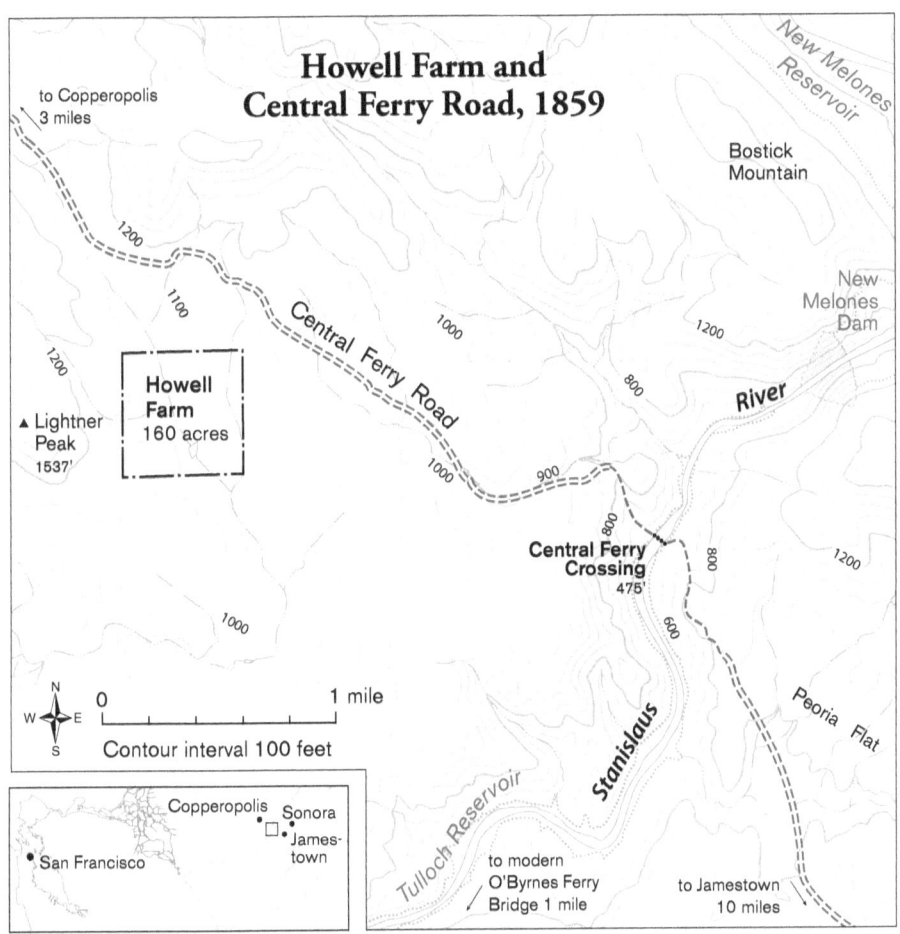

an introduction to that pretty girl. So I finally got to the house and knocked on the door. Mr. Howell came to the door, and I commenced to tell him my tale of woe. In the meantime, he invited me to come in and sit down.

I did not see the girl anywhere. We talked along and, finally, she came out in the room and I was introduced. I think the reason she did not come in the room sooner was because she was trying to look nice when she came in. She surely accomplished her object, for I thought she was the sweetest looking girl on earth. It was summertime. She had a white dress on. Her heavy head of hair was beautifully arranged, and everything about her was perfection.

Before I left her, I invited her to take a ride with me the following Sunday. Peaches were ripe then, and the following Sunday we drove out to Gastlin's Peach Orchard[60] and had a fine time. Six months after that we were engaged. Would have been engaged sooner, but I had to cut out another fellow, and it took a little time to settle his hash. Soon after I was engaged.

I built a cottage near my store. There was a family living about two miles from me. They were going to leave and had advertised to sell out at auction. They had some nice things in the way of furniture. So I attended the auction. I bought a number of things. They had a self-rocking cradle. It would wind up like a clock and run twelve hours. That was put up at auction. I thought it would be a good speculation on my part so I bid on it and brought it home with my other things.

You ought to have heard the joshing that I got for buying a self-rocking cradle before I was married. At all events, it proved to be the best bargain I ever made in the way of furniture. When it was wound up, it clicked like a clock. Put the baby in it and start it to run and that click would put it to sleep right away—a marvelous assistance to the Mother. It more than paid for all the joshing I got when I brought it home. That cradle business is surely very amusing. I know Edith[61] will laugh.

JACOB FIGHTS A THIEF

I have two little incidents to relate at Salt Spring Valley. One day a stranger came into the store and wanted a sack of flour on credit. I told him he was a stranger to me, and if he wanted flour, he would have to pay cash for it. The pile of flour was close by, and he walked over to it and said he would take a sack anyway. I jumped over the counter, and, as I did that, he drew a knife on me and before he had time to use it, I hit him right under the ear, knocking him down and, by the time I got through with him, he was glad to leave my store without a sack of flour.

I hurt myself nearly as much as I hurt him. By hitting him the first blow, I broke my large thumb joint on my left hand. It pained me awfully and was a long time getting well. However, it was a lucky blow for me. For a day or so later, I learned he was a desperado and a very bad character all around. Had I not knocked him down, something serious might have happened to me, as he had his dirk knife already in his hand.

A few days later, a word came to me that he had been killed by his partner that was living with him in a cabin about two miles from my store. They were quarreling and his partner took his rifle and shot him dead. That was good news to me, for had he lived I might have had trouble with him later on.

HE OUTWITS A CONSTABLE

I used to sell a good deal of charcoal at my store. I hired a man to burn me a kiln. After he had burned it, I found out he was selling some and putting the money in his pocket. I called him down for it, and he gave me some sauce, and I gave him a few light thumps and discharged him. Next day, he went up to Angels Camp twelve miles from my place and swore out a warrant against me for assault and battery.

Now I was very busy and did not have time to go to Angels Camp before the Justice Court. I had to get up some scheme to get out of it. The following day, the day I knew the warrant would be served, I had a load of goods to deliver to the miners on the Stanislaus River. I told my clerk that the Constable would be here with a warrant for me. Also, told him I would not be back from the river until late, and I could not lose a day to go to Angels Camp.

My clerk's name was John Quinn. I says to him, "Now, John, when that Constable comes, I want you to tell him I will not be home until late in the afternoon and you and the boys around the store get him full [drunk]." John says, "All right, I know what you mean." He says, "That guy won't have any warrant for you when you get home."

I arrived home about four o'clock and found the Constable so full, he could hardly walk, and, while in that condition, the boys had taken the warrant from his pocket. John in the meantime told me the thing was all fixed, and "you will not be served with any warrant." After I had put up my horses, I went into the store. The Constable came up to me and he says, "Mr. Pike, I have a warrant for you." I says, "If that is so, shin it out to me." You ought to have seen him going through his pockets trying to find the warrant.

Finally, he gave up. He said he must have lost it on the road. I says, if you was as drunk when you left home as you are now, I am surprised you found the way here. He returned to Angels Camp without his prisoner. That was a good many years ago. I guess he got home to Angels Camp all right. Never have seen him since. Neither did the warrant ever come to light. Very unfortunate circumstances for the Angels Camp Constable. An Officer cannot accomplish any business when he is drunk (Moral).

JACOB AND MARY ARE MARRIED

1860, Ages–Jacob 29, Mary 18

I was married at my wife's home[62] November 25, 1860.[63] Had a great wedding. Started in my buggy for Stockton. From there we took a steamboat for San Francisco. Was gone only a week on my honeymoon. I had my house ready and furnished to move into. We were fixed up quite cozy and were happy.

COPPEROPOLIS BOOMS

1861, Ages–Jacob 30, Mary 19

The copper mines were discovered the first part of 1861. Our Civil War commenced in 1861. That was the cause of copper[64] advancing very much. I saw a good opportunity for business at the copper mines. The town was Copperopolis two-and-a-half miles from where I was located. I set about getting a purchaser for my store in Salt Spring Valley, and I soon found one.

I moved to Copperopolis.[65] Built a store and a house for self & wife. Built my store which at that time was the first store in the town[66] and had it stocked with general merchandise in thirty days.[67] I was appointed postmaster[68] and an agent for Wells Fargo & Co. Had a flourishing business right from the start. The different mines were working one thousand men and other stores were starting.[69] But I, being the first one there, had the advantage. Being postmaster and Wells Fargo agent gave me great prestige.

My first born, C. W. Pike, was born in Copperopolis Nov. 13th, 1861. Here is where my self-rocking cradle came into play. You remember I mentioned it in previous memories. I bought it on speculation, and it was not very long before it demonstrated its usefulness.

I located a copper claim about seven miles from Copperopolis, and it opened very well. I shipped quite a little ore from it. Was offered $20,000 for it, but copper was high, and I refused the offer which proved to me a great mistake.

COPPEROPOLIS BUSTS

1865, Ages–Jacob 34, Mary 23

For in 1865, the [Civil] War closed, and the price of copper went [dropped] out of sight in price,[70] and the mines closed down. In consequence, the whole town was busted. And it has never been anything since. I had a good deal of property in town, but it was worth nothing after the crash.

I forgot to mention that I spent a good deal of money on my mine in the way of improvements, such as sinking and timbering, shaft engine, wire rope, engine house, and a large boarding and sleeping house for men at the mine. After the crash came, they were not worth ten cents on the dollar. About a year before the War closed, I sold out my store, and, when the crash came, I was building a brick building. Had it about completed and did intend to open a clothing store. But all my plans were blown to the four winds of heaven with everybody leaving town for new fields.

I went to San Francisco and engaged to work for B. C. Horn & Co.[71] as a drummer [salesman] in the tobacco and cigar business. I rented a house and sent for my family to come to San Francisco.[72] When I got them nicely settled, I started for the road.

SACRAMENTO TO PORTLAND BY STAGECOACH

1866, Age 35

There were four of us representing different lines of goods. (This is now 1866.) We went to Sacramento and took the stage for Portland, Oregon, a distance of over six hundred miles.[73] We drummed every town on the road, and there were many from Sacramento to Portland. We were about six weeks making it, and, when we arrived in Portland, we were a tired set of boys. We all did an excellent business. We were the first drummers that ever took that trip straight through by stage.

We had a good rest in Portland, and from there we went to Tacoma, Seattle, and Victoria. From there home by steamer. We were gone about two-and-a-half months on the trip. All the firms congratulated each of their men for making a very successful and profitable trip. My boss was only giving me one hundred and twenty-five dollars a month. I struck him for a raise, and he declined to pay any more.

Drummers on a stagecoach trip from Sacramento to Portland, 1866.
From l. to r., Jacob Pike (tobacco & cigars), Dick Brainard (drugs),
Jim Riley (shoes), and Joe Schroder (hardware).

SALT LAKE CITY MISSION

A few days afterward, Mr. Weil of Weil & Co.,[74] who by the way was the largest wholesale Tobacco & Cigar house in the city, came to me and says, "I hear your party that made the trip from Sacramento to Portland had a very profitable trip." I said, "Yes, we did very well." He says to me, "The wholesale merchants of this city are getting up a board of trade to go to Salt Lake City to solicit trade, and I will give you two hundred a month and expenses to represent our house in the Salt Lake City board of trade."

I says, "I will accept it. When do you want me to come to work?" He says, "You can come to work tomorrow if you wish." I told him I would be on hand tomorrow morning. Went to work as agreed. It took us several days for the board to get ready. When every arrangement was made, we started for Salt Lake City.

FINDING BROTHER GEORGE

Right here I want to mention about meeting my brother George, who I had not seen for over thirty years. He had been a railroad engineer for many years. I had heard a short time before he was working for the Union Pacific, running a train into Ogden, Utah. So when we arrived at Ogden, I enquired of a Union Pacific Engineer (as Ogden was the terminus of that line) if he knew an Engineer by the name of George Pike. He said, "I do, and he is in town now. You will probably find him at the hotel uptown."

I skinned out for the hotel. I enquired of the proprietor if a man by the name of George Pike was stopping in there. He said he was. I told him I was his brother and would like to see him. He looked out of the door and said there he is coming across the square in front of the hotel. I walked and met him. I says, "I understand your name is George Pike." He said it was. I said, "My name is J. M. Pike, your brother," and a loving match came off right there.

He went to Salt Lake with me and stayed with me a week, about all the time I was there. A short time after that he came to San Francisco and worked for Southern Pacific and from there went to Oregon for the same company and had charge of a construction train. By mistake of the train dispatcher, he was killed by collision.[75] His engine turned over on top of him. Before they got to him, the poor fellow was dead. He is buried at Vancouver, Washington.[76]

BRIGHAM YOUNG'S BALL
1870, Age 39

We all had a fine time in Salt Lake City. All made good connections with the merchants.[77] Brigham Young invited all of us to one of his balls and introduced us to his daughters, numbering about forty. With a very few exceptions, all were fine looking. It is against their rules to dance round dances. So we were compelled to dance the old fashion Cotillions, and you bet we made those fat Mormon girls fly around until twelve o'clock that night, as that was the time they always close their dancing.

It is putting it very mild to say we had one hilarious time. All of us thanked Brigham Young for the honor he had bestowed on us. We looked upon it as an honor, for we were told that very seldom does Brigham Young invite gentiles to his dances. The next day we were invited to visit the Mormon Tabernacle. That surely is a wonderful structure. I forget now the number of people it holds, but it runs into the thousands. I understand they have the largest organ in the world.

We were there ten days, and all of us were treated royally. All had done a very good business and we all left Salt Lake City with kind remembrances in our hearts for Salt Lake City. On our way home, we visited several cities in Nevada, which were very prosperous at that time in 1867. We arrived in San Francisco after about four weeks absent. The firms we represented all congratulated us on our successful trip.

NEW YORK BAKERY AND RESTAURANT

I worked for Weil & Co. up to the middle of 1870. They were fine people. Could not have asked to have been treated better. Every Christmas I was with them, they gave me two hundred dollars. They had a man working for them before I went in their employ. He left them and bought a half interest in the New York Bakery and Restaurant,[78] corner of Kearny and Clay Street. His health had failed some. He had made a good deal of money. He made a proposition to me to buy his interest in the Bakery & Restaurant. Knowing it was a money maker, I made arrangements to buy him out for $10,000 with a small amount down and the balance to be paid out of the profits of the business. So I left Weil & Co.'s employ and took possession of my purchase.

A man by the name of O. D. Baldwin[79] was my partner. We made money very fast, and, in a very short time, I made enough money to pay for my interest in the business, and, shortly after, I bought out my partner O. D. Baldwin.[80]

UNITED STATES RESTAURANT

1873, Age 42

The first of 1873, I bought a large restaurant called the United States Restaurant,[81] at the corner of Clay & Montgomery, and ran them both. My profits that year were sixty thousand dollars. The business in both restaurants was enormous. Used to give out in both restaurants about five thousand meals a day.[82] Made money very fast.

In 1875, I opened a wholesale grocery house[83] on the corner of Davis and California Street and took in two partners, young men who had experience in the grocery business. Allowed them one quarter each in the profits, and I furnished the capital.

Jacob Pike, about 1876.

CROSS-COUNTRY CENTENNIAL TRIP

1876, Ages–Jacob 45, Mary 34

On May 1st, 1876, I took my wife and two children (Charlie[84] and Laura[85]) to attend the Centennial.[86] I went to St. Louis first and from there went to Arkansas to visit my wife's folks. That was a great treat for her, for she never had seen any of them since 1852. We had an elegant visit of two weeks.[87]

From there we visited Washington [D.C.]. Were there three days and took in all the sights. From there we went to Baltimore and from Baltimore to Boston, from Boston to Eastport, my old native town, where we were most welcomed.[88] We more than enjoyed ourselves with our Mother,[89] Sister,[90] and all relations. Was there about four weeks.

Mary Pike, about 1878.

I had engaged my room in Philadelphia for four weeks. We arrived there July 2nd, got settled in, and commenced to take in the sights. It was so hot and so many people, I told my wife I would never be able to stay there four weeks, for I never was in such a jam of people, and the hot weather night and day was unbearable.[91] My wife thought the same as I, for the poor thing would sit up in the bed all night and fan herself.

We stayed there ten days. The last day I was there, I came very near having sun stroke. So we concluded, while we were able, to get out. It would be best to do so. We put out for home as fast as the good Lord would let us. I never can forget our experience in Philadelphia at the Centennial in 1876.

FINANCIAL PANIC STRIKES SAN FRANCISCO
1877, Age 46

We arrived home in good health. When we started for the East, I was offered twenty thousand [dollars] for the U.S. Restaurant and declined to sell, which was another mistake of mine. I paid twelve thousand for it, and, when I left for the East, the business was not as good as it used to be.

Just before I started on my trip, I figured up what I was worth. It was $140,000, including real estate, money I had in stocks, the grocery business, two restaurants, and cash on hand. When I returned, things were in pretty bad shape. The bottom had fallen out of the restaurant business, and my grocery business was not very thrifty. The two young men I took on as partners did not seem to be a success. They were good salesmen, but their management was poor. Being proprietors, they both got the big head and it spoiled them. I got rid of one right away. Finally, in a few months, I sold out with a big loss.

Also, the bottom had fallen out of stocks, of which I had a large number of shares in the Nevada mines.[92] I went to my broker's office and requested him to sell every share of stock I had, but not in a day. For so large a block of stock would break the market from what it was then. He sold it all in three days. A lucky thing I did, for in a few days it went much lower. After I got my statement from my broker, I figured up what I lost in all my stock dealings. I was a seventy-thousand-dollar loser.

A short time after that, my broker failed. The stock market broke him flat, and, to make the matter still worse, I and another man were on his note for twenty thousand dollars in his bank. The other man that was on the note with me, put his property out of his hands and left me to pay it all. I compromised with the bank by paying them ten thousand dollars.

I worked out of this scrape honorably and went to work vigorously to make more money. Those were terrible times. A great many of my friends lost everything they had and never did recuperate. But such blows as I have here narrated always gave me more energy. I guess that is the reason I have lived to be a good old age.

I had already sold my restaurants before I had sold my grocery store.

CIGAR FACTORY FAILS

1881, Age 50

It is now 1881. I opened a cigar factory on Battery Street.[93] Charlie was then twenty years old. I took him in with me as a partner and did most of the drumming, while he drummed in California and Oregon. We did very well. But Charlie wanted to go into Colorado and Texas. So he took that country in, and the result was we lost in bad accounts six thousand [dollars].

That crippled me very much, as my capital was small. Charlie was married in 1882 or 1883. I did not like the idea, he being too young, about 21 years. Soon after he was married, he drew out from me and went into the commission business. A short time after that, I sold my factory to my bookkeeper, Mr. _____ . I have forgotten his name now.

JACOB BUYS ANOTHER RESTAURANT

I again went into the bakery & restaurant business. Bought out Swain's Bakery & Restaurant[94] on Market Street opposite the Palace Hotel. This was not like old times, although I did a very fair business until the unions interfered with us. Closed me up one time for a week. They had no grievances against me. It was a sympathetic strike. So I had to suffer for another's wrongdoings.

Most of the restaurant proprietors of the main restaurants in the city got together and formed a society and pledged ourselves not to employ a union man in our business. We so advertised in the papers, and, in a very short time, we engaged enough non-union men for our wants and opened for business. We were the cause of breaking up the restaurant union at that time and did not have any more trouble as long as I was in the business. But our losses were considerable before we opened up. In two months, my business was as good as it was before the strike.

In 1889 there was a man running a restaurant about half a block away on Market Street. The property was sold, and he had to move. He came to me and wanted to buy my place. He offered me a pretty good price for it, so I sold it to him. A year later, I bought a half interest in Manning's Oyster House and Restaurant,[95] right opposite Baldwin's Hotel on Powell Street.

MARY DIES

1892, Ages–Jacob 61, Mary 50

A short time after that, on April 17th, 1892, my wife died.[96] With all the bad luck I had through life, that was the hardest blow on me. My children, four boys and one girl, were my responsibilities,[97] and I have tried hard to do my duty toward them. I know, with the exception of one, my goodness to them is appreciated, and may they forever prosper.

After I had been in the business on Powell Street about two years, rent commenced to raise. My necessary expenses had been very great in the last two years on account of sickness and family expenses and with larger rents, I found it pretty hard to make it go.

YOSEMITE INNKEEPER

In the spring of 1895, Mr. Cook[98] wanted me to go to Yosemite with him and manage his hotel[99] on a salary. I was in debt in the restaurant and had to compromise with my creditors. I paid them fifty cents on the dollar, and they gave me a receipt in full of all demands. I accepted Mr. Cook's proposition and went to Yosemite Valley with him. We did a fine business that summer. Always closed the hotel in the winter by the middle of November.

TYNAN HOTEL, MODESTO
1895–1911, Age 64–80

I came home via Modesto. Stayed there a few days and looked around for business. There was a German keeping the Tynan Hotel.[100] He was doing no business to speak of. Mr. Tynan owned everything in the house with exception of the kitchen, dining room, office, and bar room furniture. He wanted me to buy out the German. Mr. Tynan said he thought he would sell, as he was doing no business to speak of. So I tackled him and bought him out.

I paid him something to bind the bargain and told him I would have to go to San Francisco to settle some business and would be there in ten days to take possession. I was on hand at the time stated and paid him for his stuff. He only had five hundred dollars' worth. Got my lease from Mr. Tynan for two years at $125.00 per month. You bet I went to work in earnest.

Jacob Pike in Modesto, 1903

There was another hotel in town, an old wooden building and had about all the drummer trade. It was called Ross House.[101] I attended every train, and in six months I had all the drummer trade as well as the town trade. Very soon the Ross House burnt down. So I had it all to myself in the way of business and commenced to make money now.

I ran it eight years. In the meantime, Mr. Tynan died and from that time on I had to deal with his wife. Of course, as my business increased, my rent was at the end of the eight years $200.00 per month. Mrs. Tynan notified me at the expiration of my lease she would give it to her son-in-law. So I had to step down and out. Mr. Duncan, her son-in-law, paid me for what I had in the house, but not near what it cost me. Well, he ran the hotel twenty-two months.

In 1897, I bought 240 acres of land six miles from Modesto. After I left the hotel, I went on my ranch and commenced improving it. After I finished improving it and, as I said before, he [the son-in-law] had been in the hotel twenty-two months, he drank and gambled a good deal and neglected his business, his wife got after him to sell out. I heard that and approached him on the subject. He had made some new improvements which were very necessary.

I finally bought him out for $4,000.00 cash. It was a big price for what he had. The town was improving very fast, and I knew I could do a good business. So I did not care if I did pay more than it was worth. I got a lease for three years at $250.00 per month, and it was extended twice.

One year ago, the first of last August [1911], I again had to step down and out.[102] My lease was up, and Mrs. Tynan gave it to her son. He fell from grace also after three months. He too commenced drinking heavily. She put him out of the house. She and her daughter are running it now and are doing very well.

JACOB PREPARES HIS WILL

I would have liked to have kept it a little longer. When I went out, was making $1,000.00 a month. However, I have enough now to keep me as long as I live. When I pass away, there will be enough to make a fine dividend between my four sons: Willis, Tom, Roy, and Percy. My son Charles[103] has plenty. Also, my daughter[104] has ample means [and this] is the reason I do not name them in my "Will."

THE HOWELL FAMILY

Mr. James Howell & wife & family started from Russellville, Arkansas, with his family in ox team for California in 1852. Stayed all winter in Salt Lake City. Arrived in California at Woodbridge, about twelve miles east of Stockton, I think it was, the latter part of 1853. Their family consists of:

Nancy	Now Mrs. Edminson
Mary Lucy	Now dead [Jacob's wife]
Thos. Howell	Now dead
George Howell	
Henry Howell	
Vandalia	Now Mrs. Hudelson
Hains Howell	
George Howell	
Viola	Now Mrs. McKay
Alice born in California	Now Mrs. Peeler of Coalinga

Vandalia, now Mrs. Hudelson, is a triplet, one died soon after birth. The other lived to be twelve years old. Vandalia is a fine healthy woman. She has five children. The two boys are married, and Albert leases my ranch. Both fine boys. None of the girls are married and better girls never lived than they.

The Howell family moved on a ranch in Calaveras about six miles from Copperopolis in 1858. Right there is the place I found the best wife that ever lived. It was worth more than one horse to find her. I chided myself so often that I did not listen to her counsel. If I had, I would have been worth over a million today. I did what I thought was for the best, but could not see so far ahead as she.

However, in the last fifteen years, I made up some of my lost fortune. The way in taking so many chances as I have of my life, I thank God that I have attained the age I am, now past 80 years old.

THE J. M. PIKE FAMILY

J. M. Pike married to Mary Lucy Howell Nov. 25, 1860

Charles W. Pike	born Nov. 13, 1861 in Copperopolis
Laura Celia Pike	born Jul. 14, 1863 in Copperopolis
J. M. Pike Jr.	born Jul. 16, 1865 in Copperopolis, d. Jul. 24, 1867
Fred Harald Pike	born Sep. 11, 1868 in San Francisco, d. Nov. 14, 1869
James Howell Pike	born Aug. 18, 1870 in San Francisco, d. Jun. 25, 1871
Willis Pike	born Jul. 6, 1872 in San Francisco
Thos. Howell Pike	born Jul. 4, 1874 in San Francisco
Roy Melville Pike	born Feb. 10, 1878 in San Francisco
Percy Mortimer Pike	born Sep. 25, 1882 in San Francisco

ADDENDUM TO THE MEMOIRS OF J. M. PIKE

Note: The author of this typed addendum is unknown. Evidence suggests that it was written circa 1961 by a person knowledgeable about the history of mining on river bars on the Tuolumne and Stanislaus Rivers. The original copy is at the Bancroft Library, University of California, Berkeley.

1. SAN JOAQUIN CITY was situated where the present Durham Ferry and River Roads intersect. There is a monument marking the site. At the time of Pike's arrival there, it was the head of navigation on the San Joaquin River, although later, within a year or so, the steamers were running to Graysonville [Grayson or Grayson City] and Tuolumne City with the Lode-bound miners. Having landed on the west side of the river, it is quite possible that they crossed either at Turner's Ferry at the mouth of the Tuolumne River, or they may have crossed at the Grayson Ferry. From there they could start cross country to Sparks Ferry. San Joaquin City had a Post Office from July 28, 1851 until January 12, 1852. It was reopened on Sept. 18, 1874 but was moved to Vernalis on Dec. 11, 1888 when that town was founded on the new railroad.

2. SPARK'S FERRY was on the Tuolumne River about 1/2 mile above French Bar, now known as La Grange.

3. ROGER'S BAR was apparently about 1/2 mile above, or upstream from Don Pedro's Bar, where the present-day Roger's Creek empties into the Tuolumne.

4. BIG OAK FLAT appears on all modern maps. It has had a Post Office since Jan. 21, 1852. Pike's reference to the amount of rain, or rather the lack of it, is interesting. According to records kept at Sacramento, that season, i.e., July, 1850 to July, 1851, there was recorded only 4.71 inches, whereas the year before they had 36 inches and the year after 17.98. I believe that the year when he was at Big Oak Flat is probably the driest year of record.

5. STEPHENSON'S BAR. Probably intended as STEVENS' BAR. It is where the present highway between Jacksonville and Big Oak Flat crosses the Tuolumne River. This bridge has always been known as Stevens' Bar Bridge.

6. HAWKIN'S BAR was about 1/2 mile below, or downstream from, the town of Jacksonville. This was where the first activity on the Tuolumne River began. 15 men started operations on this bar in April 1849. By that same year the bar had a population of 700 persons.

7. MORGAN'S BAR I cannot definitely locate except that it was above Don Pedro's Bar.

8. DON PEDRO'S BAR was about 1/4 mile above the present Don Pedro Dam. It survived the longest of any of the river bars. It had a Post Office from Nov. 22, 1853 until April 3, 1866. It is said that in the Presidential election of 1860 Don Pedro's Bar cast a total of 1500 votes. It was a rich bar, as one claim alone yielded $100,000 by 1889, at a cost of only $5,000.

9. INDIAN BAR, as Pike says, apparently lay next above or upstream from Morgan's Bar.

10. MONTEZUMA is now a ghost town. It was situated about 3 miles south of Jamestown on the old road to Chinese Camp. The junction of this old road and the present highway is about 2 miles northeast of what is known as Yosemite Junction. The old junction is still called Montezuma Junction, although the town stood about a mile or less south of this point. Montezuma had a Post Office from March 31, 1854 until March 8, 1887, when it was moved to Chinese Camp. The last time I saw it [the town], about 1952 or thereabouts, there was only one old residence left and a small cemetery nearby. The residence was remodeled from the Fox General Merchandise store.

11. NASTY BAR. I can find no reference to this bar in any of the standard histories.

ADDENDUM MAP: TUOLUMNE RIVER BARS

LEGEND: 2. Spark's Ferry, 3. Roger's Bar, 4. Big Oak Flat, 5. Stevens' Bar, 6. Hawkins' Bar, 7. Morgan's Bar, 8. Don Pedro's Bar, 9. Indian Bar, 10. Montezuma, A. Red Mountain Bar, B. Swett's Bar.

NOTE: This is a portion (4.75 x 5.25 inches) of the Addendum Map (8.5 x 11 inches), which was cut out from the bottom left-hand corner of a larger map, probably a U.S. Forest Service map circa 1950. (The darkened outline of the U.S. Forest border is visible in the top right-hand corner.) The pattern of one-mile squares across the map are sections ordered by township and range from the Mount Diablo Base Line and Meridian. The original Addendum Map is in the Bancroft Library, University of California, Berkeley.

12. GRAND BAR I find mentioned, but not located, in Tuolumne County histories. The shooting scrape in which Warren was killed is mentioned in one history as having started at Grand Bar and that it took place Aug. 4, 1858. This date does not jibe with Pike's account. When he said Morgan's Bar, I am sure he meant Grand Bar.

13. LOUGHEAD [LAWHEAD] FERRY. I can find no reference to this ferry, although it may have been an early name for one of the numerous ferries on the Stanislaus River. [It was the Central Ferry, owned by Mr. Lawhead; see endnote 47 on page 54.]

14. COULTERVILLE appears on all modern maps, and it has had a typical Mother Lode type of history since its founding.

15. SALT SPRING VALLEY lies 5 miles northwest of Copperopolis on the road to Milton. It had a Post Office from April 17, 1878 to May 24, 1880. A little settlement, more recently known as Towers, is in all probability the same place, but renamed for the principal landowner in the area.

16. ANGELS CAMP appears on all modern maps.

17. COPPEROPOLIS is now almost a ghost town, although it revived to some extent during World War II when copper mines were partially reopened to supply our war needs. With the close of the war and the decline in the price of copper, the town again was almost deserted. The Post Office was established on Dec. 19, 1861.

18. THE TYNAN HOTEL stands at the northwest corner of 10th and H Streets, in Modesto. It has borne the name of "State Hotel" for the past few years. At the time it was built in 1891, it was the first hotel in the area to have an elevator and also to be wired for electricity. It is presently being torn down as it did not qualify as a "safe" building under present codes.

19. THE ROSS HOUSE stood at the southeast corner of 9th and I Street on the site now occupied by the Claremont Hotel, which was built in 1905. It is also doomed to be destroyed under our so-called "Safe Building" code. The Ross House was a two-story wooden structure built about 1867 or '68 in Paradise City by Frank H. Ross. This old river town was located at Grimes and Paradise Roads, about 2 miles west of Modesto. It was founded by John Mitchell in 1867. When Modesto was founded in 1871, Ross moved the entire building to the new town.

ENDNOTES

A BOY'S LIFE IN MAINE

1   In family lore, the spelling of Jacob Pike's middle name has remained elusive. His gravestone in the Woodlawn Cemetery in Colma, CA, spells it "Maybe." But Jacob registered to vote in California on numerous occasions giving his middle name as "Mabee." (San Francisco County Voter Registers: 1869, 1872, 1876, 1880, 1882, 1886, 1888, 1890, 1892; Stanislaus County: 1896), and he signed a published "Notice of Copartnership" as "Jacob Mabee Pike," *Daily Alta California*, Mar. 9, 1878, 2.

2   Jacob incorrectly wrote that he was seven and his father, Captain William Pike, thirty-five when he died. In fact, Jacob was five and his father thirty-three. See Death notice in the *Columbian Centinel* (Boston): "Pike, William, Capt., of Eastport, lost overboard from fishing schr., *Swiftsure*, in Little River, Oct. 25th, age 33 (*C.C.*, Nov. 5, 1836)." Source: Ancestry.com: U.S., Newspaper Extractions from the Northeast, 1704–1930 / Massachusetts / Columbian Centinel / Death / Surname: Pabodie-Roane / page 409 of 924. Little River is a headland on Passamaquoddy Bay near Eastport, Maine.

3   Jacob was the middle child. His four siblings were Samuel Tuttle (b. 1826, d. 1915), George K. (b. 1828, d. 1883), William (b. 1834, d. unknown), and Helen Ann, also known as Celia, (b. 1837, m. George H. Paine abt. 1854, d. 1929).

4   Probably enumerated as "Purtmon Haughton" in 1850, as "Portman Houghton" in 1860, and as "P. Houghton" in 1870 in the U.S. Census for Eastport, Washington County, Maine.

5   A bark is a vessel of three or more masts, fore-and-aft rigged on the aftermost one and fully square-rigged on the remainder. Source: Harold A. Underhill, *Sailing Ship Rigs and Rigging* (Glasgow: Brown, Son & Ferguson, Ltd.), 3.

6   Possibly "William Dunham" enumerated in Eastport, Washington County, Maine in the 1850 Census.

7   A brig is a two-masted vessel, fully square-rigged on both masts. Source: Harold A. Underhill, *Sailing Ship Rigs and Rigging* (Glasgow: Brown, Son & Ferguson, Ltd.), 6.

8   A small village at the mouth of the Chagres River, the largest river in Panama. Early in the Gold Rush, Chagres was the principal port on the east coast of Panama, later replaced by Aspinwall (modern Colón).

9   A malignant malarial fever occurring along the Chagres River in Panama. Source: *Merriam-Webster*.

GOLD RUSH BOUND
1849, Age 18

10   In his handwritten memoir, Jacob identified his ship as the *Nathan Hooper*, which was later incorrectly transcribed in a privately printed family memoir as the *Nathan Hopper*. The correct full name was *Nathaniel Hooper*.

   The *Nathaniel Hooper* had three masts, all square-rigged. Tons: 427, Type: Ship, Year Built: 1837, Place Built: Newbury, Mass., Registered in New York: July 11, 1848. Source: *List of American-Flag Merchant Vessels that Received Certificates of Enrollment or Registry at the Port of New York, 1789–1867, Volume II* (Special Lists, Number 22, Washington, DC: National Archives, 1968), 500.

11   The *Nathaniel Hooper* departed Eastport on July 10, 1849. Jacob turned eighteen six weeks later on August 23, 1849.

12   "Although now a responsible watch officer, living aft in [Richard Henry] Dana's 'world of knives and forks' and called 'Mister' by the mate and the captain and 'Sir' by the men, he was still part sailor and expected to lay aloft to reef and furl and to dip his hand in the tar bucket. Mistrusted by the forecastle and but tolerated by the mate and the captain, he was neither fish nor fowl." W. H. Bunting, *Live Yankees:*

The Sewalls and Their Ships (Gardiner, ME: Tilbury House, 2009), 37. See pages 36–41 for a description of the relationships between the captain, first mate, and second mate.

MUTINY AT SEA

13 "The line between enforcement of necessary discipline and tyranny was sometimes hard to distinguish, as was the line between sane, but severe, and psychotic captains and mates." Ibid., 39. See also Elmo Paul Hohman, *History of American Merchant Seamen* (Hamden, CT: Shoe String Press, 1956), 25.

14 St. Catherine's was Santa Catarina Island off the coast of Brazil. "Many skippers preferred St. Catherine's, which had long been a stopping place for American whalers, and which had a good harbor, excellent water, and ample supplies of wood and fruit. Moreover, it was more nearly on their course than Rio and promised less delay than they were likely to encounter in that crowded harbor." Oscar Lewis, *Sea Routes to the Gold Fields: The Migration by Water to California in 1849–1852* (New York: Alfred A. Knopf, 1949), 125. For an overview of St. Catherine's, see his chapter three, section 1, pp. 125–131.

15 See *U.S. Consular Records for Santa Catarina, Brazil, compiled 1834–1874 from Records of the Foreign Service Posts of the Department of State*. National Archives, Record Group 84, Entry UD 795, vols. 3 and 5. Testimony from passengers and crew of the *Nathaniel Hooper* was taken on or after Aug. 21, 1849.

16 Jacob wrote "SE gale" (southeast gale). He must have meant a SW (southwest) gale. The prevailing winds at Cape Horn are westerly, which is why rounding from east to west is so difficult. Ocean winds are described by the direction from which they come. Currents are described by the direction toward which they flow.

MIRACULOUS FALL OFF A YARDARM

17 Jacob wrote that he arrived on February 10. But the *Daily Alta California* reported that the *Nathaniel Hooper* arrived on Feb. 4, 1850, under Captain "Griffin, 235 days from New York, with 5 passengers." *Daily Alta California*, Feb. 5, 1850, 3. Although registered in New York, the ship had sailed from Maine.

Nineteen days later, the ship's captain placed an advertisement in the *Daily Alta California*: "Cargo of ship 'Nathaniel Hooper,' from New York—230,000 feet undressed lumber, best quality and of all sizes, 50,000 feet assorted scantling, 26,000 feet hemlock boards, 70,000 best shingles. For sale entire or buy in lots, by E. MICKLE & Co., Clay Street wharf." *Daily Alta California*, Feb. 23, 1850, 3. Note to researchers: If browsing the California Digital Newspaper Collection, Saturday issues of the *Daily Alta California* are listed as published on Sunday; so the Feb. 23 issue is listed as Feb. 24.

BROTHER SAM SURPRISES JACOB
1850, Age 19

18   Samuel Pike took the faster steamer route to California via the Isthmus of Panama. George H. Tinkham, *History of Stanislaus County, California: With Biographical Sketches* (Los Angeles: Historic Record Co., 1921), 809.

19   The boat carrying Jacob and Sam likely landed at the Central Wharf, which one early resident described as the heart of the city. It "was the thoroughfare for communication with vessels, and was crowded from morning 'til night with drays and wagons coming and going; sailors, miners, and others of all nationalities, speaking with a great variety of tongues, moved busily about; steamers arriving and departing; schooners were taking merchandise for the mines; boats were crowding in here and there—the whole resembling a great beehive, where at first glance everything appeared to be noise, confusion, and disorder." James P. Delgado, *Gold Rush Port: The Maritime Archaeology of San Francisco's Waterfront* (Berkeley: University of California Press, 2009), 58.

20   Located on Pacific, near Sansome Street, the Maine Hotel was "a house…40 feet front by 25 feet deep, two stories, made in New York, of the best materials, and in every respect well built." *Daily Alta California*, Jan 11, 1850, 3.

21   The name *Raven* does not match the historical record. Although a British brig named *Raven* did visit San Francisco in July 1850, Jacob was already gold mining on the Tuolumne River at this time. Source: *Daily Alta California*, Jul. 3, 1850, p. 2, and Jul. 22, 1850, p. 3. The following year, Jacob was back in San Francisco and might have worked on the clipper ship *Raven*, which arrived from Boston on November 19, 1851. Source: *Daily Alta California*, Nov. 22, 1851, 2.

SEARCHING FOR GOLD

22 The "Southern Mines" referred to those mines in the Sierra foothills drained by the San Joaquin River, including the Stanislaus and Tuolumne Rivers. Susan Lee Johnson, *Roaring Camp: The Social World of the California Gold Rush* (New York: W. W. Norton & Company, 2000), 11–12.

23 See *Addendum to the Memoirs of J. M. Pike*, #1 San Joaquin City. Mildred Brook Hoover, et al., *Historic Spots in California*, 5th ed., rev. by Douglas E. Kyle (Stanford: Stanford University Press, 2002), 378: "A settlement was started on the west side of the San Joaquin River a little below the mouth of the Stanislaus [River]. Hoping to become a rival of Stockton, San Joaquin City, as it was called then, persisted for a number of years…Nothing but a historic plaque marks the location today, on County Road J-3 1.4 miles north of the Stanislaus county line." On Google Maps, this would be near the intersection of Durham Ferry Road / Airport Way & Kasson Road, opposite 31167 Kasson Road, Tracy.

24 Jacob wrote the "Tuolumne River," but it was the Stanislaus River.

25 See *Addendum to the Memoirs of J. M. Pike*, #2 Spark's Ferry. Spark's Ferry was located near present-day La Grange, thirty miles east of Modesto on CA-132 (Yosemite Boulevard).

26 See *Addendum to the Memoirs of J. M. Pike*, #3 Roger's Bar. Mildred Brook Hoover, et al., *Historic Spots in California*, 5th ed., rev. by Douglas E. Kyle (Stanford: Stanford University Press, 2002), 551: "During 1850 the river camps along the Tuolumne were among the largest in the county, thousands of miners being engaged in attempts to divert the river in order to mine its bed. Few of the camps, however, enjoyed any great prosperity, and all of them, Hawkins', Swett's, Stevens', Payne's, Hart's, Morgan's, Roger's, Signorita, York, and Texas Bars, have completely disappeared."

MORE BAD LUCK

27 F. J. Thibault, a miner working a claim on Indian Bar, five miles upstream, experienced a similar fate, writing to his wife on Sep. 30, 1850: "All our hopes, founded on the Tuolumne River, have proved a failure. We had our work completed and were just about taking out the gold, when it commenced raining and made a complete wreck of all the dams on the stream.—Hundreds of men are completely ruined—deeply in debt and out of funds." Quoted in Priscilla McArthur, *Arkansas in the Gold Rush* (Little Rock, AR: August House, 1986), 137.

28 See *Addendum to the Memoirs of J. M. Pike*, #4 Big Oak Flat.

29 See *Addendum to the Memoirs of J. M. Pike*, #5 Stevens' Bar.

30 See *Addendum to the Memoirs of J. M. Pike*, #7 Morgan's Bar.

31 See *Addendum to the Memoirs of J. M. Pike*, #6 Hawkins' Bar.

32 A rocker or cradle was a device that extracted gold much faster than a pan. It was a wooden container four feet long with a removable box or hopper atop one end and a series of parallel cleats on the bottom level. As gold-bearing dirt was shoveled into the hopper and water poured over it, a perforated plate under the hopper held back the rocks, allowing the lighter material to fall through the grate and wash out, leaving behind the gold flakes caught behind the cleats. J. S. Holliday, *Rush for Riches: Gold Fever and the Making of California* (Berkeley: University of California, 1999), 66–68.

33 See *Addendum to the Memoirs of J. M. Pike*, #8 Don Pedro's Bar.

34 "The fire of May 4, 1851 [was] the largest in the city's history until April 1906… The fire… raged for ten hours, destroyed between one thousand and two thousand buildings, and destroyed some $12 million in property; the city never made an accurate count of the dead." James P. Delgado, *Gold Rush Port: The Maritime Archaeology of San Francisco's Waterfront* (Berkeley: University of California Press, 2009), 80.

BACK TO THE SEA
1851, Age 20

35 The "Shipping Intelligence" column in the *Daily Alta California* mentioned the *Vincennes* on dates corresponding to Jacob's timeline. "Jun. 13, 1851–At Realejo [Nicaragua], US sloop of war *Vincennes*, Capt Hudson to sail in a few days for San Francisco via Acapulco and Mazatlan; crew all well." Arrived in San Francisco, "Aug. 4, 1851–US sloop-of-war *Vincennes*, Wm. L. Hudson, commanding, from a cruise on the coast 34 days fm Mazatlan." *Daily Alta California*, Jun. 13, 1851, 2, and Aug. 5, 1852, 2.

SEARCHING FOR GOLD, AGAIN

36 See "Mining with the Hatheway Brothers, 1854."

37 See *Addendum to the Memoirs of J. M. Pike*, #9 Indian Bar. In his story, "Mining with the Hatheway Brothers, 1854," Jacob wrote: "He [Charlie Hatheway] was then working on Indian Bar about five miles up the river from where I was working on Morgan's Bar."

ALMOST BURIED ALIVE
1854, Age 23

38 See *Addendum to the Memoirs of J. M. Pike*, #10 Montezuma. A California State Historical Landmark (No. 122) for Montezuma is located on Highway 49, 2.5 miles north of Chinese Camp, south of junction of CA-49 and CA-108. Montezuma was located between Jamestown and Jacksonville.

For the exact location of the town, see *Sonora, California, 1893*, U.S.G.S. map #299649 at http://nationalmap.gov/historical/.

39 See *Addendum to the Memoirs of J. M. Pike*, #14 Coulterville.

SAM BUILDS A MINING MACHINE

40 See *Addendum to the Memoirs of J. M. Pike*, #11 Grand Bar. Grand Bar was located upriver and close to Peoria Bar on the Stanislaus River. For a list of bars on the Stanislaus River, see *Daily Alta California*, Oct. 12, 1858, 1.

41 See *Addendum to the Memoirs of J. M. Pike*, #11 Nasty Bar. In his story, "Mining with the Hatheway Brothers, 1854," Jacob wrote: "After I went to the Stanislaus River in 1854, I sent for Charlie to come to the Stanislaus River to work with me on a claim that I had located on Nasty Bar, just above my claim on Grand Bar that I had located when I first went over to the Stanislaus River."

GUNFIRE IN JACOB'S STORE
1857, Age 26

42 Frederick Lux's three-page biography references his Peoria store. "He continued doing a merchandizing business during the years 1852–3–4 in this section [Burn's Ferry on the Stanislaus River] after which he removed to Peoria in Tuolumne County, where he kept store until the year 1857." Note: Brackets original, should be Byrne's Ferry. Archives of the Society of California Pioneers.

Lux became a lifelong friend of Jacob and his future wife, Mary Howell. After her death in 1892, Lux wrote: "I sympathize with you from the fullness of my heart in the loss of your dear wife." Letter from Fred Lux to Jacob Pike, San Francisco, California, Apr. 20, 1892.

43 Peoria Bar was near the junction of the Stanislaus River and Peoria Creek, about a mile downstream from the Central Ferry. Peoria Creek empties the Peoria Basin below Peoria Mountain on the eastern side of the Stanislaus River. See *Copperopolis, California, 1916*, U.S.G.S. map #297183 at http://nationalmap.gov/historical/.

BATTLE ON THE STANISLAUS RIVER
1858, Age 27

44 Jacob wrote that the assailants were Italians, but newspaper accounts agree that the assailants were Frenchmen. The Appendix includes three contemporary accounts of the shootout. While generally confirming Jacob's description of the event, they include wildly different names of victims. Most notably, the earliest two accounts reported that Jacob was killed. Jacob placed the event on the Tuolumne River in 1855. But the historical record clearly places it on the Stanislaus River in August 1858.

a) *San Joaquin Republican* (Stockton), Aug. 7, 1858, 2:
DREADFUL AFFRAY ON THE STANISLAUS!…Leonard Shoccob was instantly killed; Abram Delay, mortally wounded, Geo Crooks, shot through

both thighs...Mr. Pike was instantly killed at the first fire, and Mr. Chas. McKenny mortally wounded...

b) *Daily Alta California* (San Francisco), Aug. 8, 1858, 1:
BLOODY AFFRAY ON THE STANISLAUS RIVER...The name of the man killed was Leonard Shoccob. The one dangerously wounded, Abram Lelay. George Crooks has three balls in his legs...Mr. Pike was killed at the first fire, and Mr. Chas. McKenney mortally wounded...[Definition of affray: a fight in a public place that disturbs the peace. Source: *Merriam-Webster*].

c) *Sacramento Daily Union*, Aug. 19, 1858, 4:
THE STANISLAUS TRAGEDY...The brother immediately fired two shots, wounding two men and killing one. One of the wounded has since died...With their guns ready cocked, they stood until the foremost came within a few feet, when they opened their murderous fire, shooting Charles McKenny in the head, (which felled him to the ground.) Rodger McKue was shot in the breast, and Robert Warren received five balls in his side, penetrating the heart.

The killed and wounded now are as follows: Killed—Leonard Shock, Abraham Delevan, and Robert Warren. Wounded Geo. J. Crooks, Chas. McKenny, and Rodger McKue. The French were armed to the teeth, while the Crooks party were entirely unarmed...This is neither the *French* nor the *American* side of this unhappy story, but a plain statement of the facts as they occurred...

John F. Zollner, of Peoria Bar, Stanislaus River.

d) Twenty-four years after the event, a short account of the incident appeared in *A History of Tuolumne County, California: Compiled from the most Authentic Records* (San Francisco: B. F. Alley, 1882), 275:
"Aug. 4, 1858: Leonard Shoeck and Abraham DeLoew killed at Grand Bar, by two Frenchmen, brothers, in a mining difficulty. The murderers fled, and being pursued by a party, fired upon them from ambush, killing Robert G. Warren and wounding two others, themselves finally evading arrest."

45 Jacob mistakenly wrote "Morgan's Bar." But he meant Grand Bar. See *Addendum to the Memoirs of J. M. Pike*, #12 Grand Bar.

46 Warren's first name was Robert, not George. *Sacramento Daily Union*, Aug. 19, 1858, 4.

47   Lawhead's Ferry was the Central Ferry. See "A Trip Through the Mines," *Stockton Independent*, Feb. 20, 1858, 2. "After a few minutes' slow ride up a steep incline, we came on the road and then hastily proceeded to Central Ferry, owned by Mr. Lawhead, who lives on the Stanislaus side [north] of the stream. The Ferry was in good repair…" Note: Jacob's handwritten "Lawhead" was mistakenly transcribed as "Loughead," in the previously printed copy of his memoir. This transcription error also appears as #13 Loughead in the *Addendum to the Memoirs of J. M. Pike*.

QUARREL LEADS TO DOUBLE MURDER

48   Jacob wrote July 4, 1855, in his memoir, but the historical record confirmed that this fight took place in 1857:

> a) *Daily Alta California*, July 15, 1857, 2.
> FATAL AFFRAY – At Peoria Flat, Tuolumne county, on the 4th [of July], an altercation between two men, named Tom Boyle and Brown, resulted in the death of a third party, named Salisbury. The *Gazette* says that they had insulted Salisbury, and Brown struck him with a pistol; Salisbury returned the blow with a stab of a Bowie-knife, in the abdomen. Brown then fired four shots at Salisbury, hitting him three times, from which wounds he died almost instantly. Boyle interfered, and after Salisbury had fallen to the ground, kicked him until he was dead. The two wounded men died in a few minutes. Boyle is now in jail charged with a crime of murder.

> b) "July 4, 1857: Two men engaged in a fight at Peoria Flat, and both were killed." *A History of Tuolumne County, California: Compiled from the most Authentic Records* (San Francisco: B. F. Alley, 1882), 273.

49   A year later, Oliphant himself was arrested for murder. See *Sacramento Daily Union*, August 25, 1858, 2.

JACOB'S SAWMILL VENTURE FAILS
1856, Age 25

50   Many years later Jacob again partnered with Uriah Nelson according to a "Notice of Copartnership" filed for "Lane, Pike & Nelson…The business of this firm is that of Canning Salmon on Fraser River, B.C., Dated, San Francisco, March 7th,

1878," signed by Charles Comstock Lane, British Columbia; Jacob Mabee Pike, San Francisco, Cal.; and Uriah Nelson, British Columbia. *Daily Alta California*, Mar. 9, 1878, 2.

51 "Agriculture in the Mountains," *California Farmer and Journal of Useful Sciences*, Aug. 22, 1856, 33: "…The mill…is now owned by Messrs. Pike, Nelson & Co. Connected with this mill is one of the best mountain farms that I have ever seen; it is a prairie of from four to five hundred acres…"

The location of the property was later described in a Sheriff's Sale notice: "Situate and being about five miles northeasterly of the village of Coulterville in the County of Mariposa, State of California, known as the Mountain Ranch, containing one hundred and sixty acres more or less, on which is a sawmill known as Greeley's Mill, being the same ranch formerly located by J. M. Aiken; also two ranches north of the above, one of which was located by Uriah Nelson, the other by Jacob Pike, the said ranches are described as follows: Commencing from Southwest corner, at a point about forty yards, Northeast of Greeley's sawmill; running thence Northerly about one mile to Longfellow's ranch, to and including Greeley's Barn; thence Southerly about one mile; thence in a direct line to the place of beginning." *Mariposa Gazette*, Jan. 19, 1867, 2.

TYING A HANGMAN'S KNOT

52 For a description of vigilante activities in Coulterville, see Catherine Coffin Phillips, *Coulterville Chronicle: The Annals of a Mother Lode Mining Town* (San Francisco: The Grabhorn Press, 1942), 129.

53 Cashman was a well-known merchant in Coulterville. "Coulterville contains several fire-proof buildings, two good hotels, two billiard saloons, a number of stores, the two principal of which are the establishments of Sullivan & Cashman and Mr. Rockwell." *Sacramento Daily Union*, Sep. 19, 1857, 3.

JACOB OPENS NEW STORE
1858, Age 27

54 See *Addendum to the Memoirs of J. M. Pike*, #15 Salt Spring Valley. In 1858, news circulated that gold had been discovered in the Salt Spring Valley, sparking a brief

gold rush. See Henry O. Mace, *Between the Rivers: A History of Early Calaveras County*, California, 2nd ed. (Murphys, CA: Paul Groh Press, 2002), 93.

55   "Pike and his associates were soon doing a brisk business with the store and blacksmith shop. His well-chosen location gave him the trade of miners, farmers, and settlers in and about the valley, as well as teamsters coming and going from the [river] ferries. Pike's store soon became the center of the New Diggings settlement, and several cabins and houses were built nearby." Willard P. Fuller Jr., Judith Marvin, and Julia G. Costello, *Madam Felix's Gold: The Story of the Madam Felix Mining District*, Calaveras County, California (Calaveras County, CA: Calaveras County Historical Society and Foothill Resources, 1996), 18. The settlement of New Diggings later became known as Hodson, which pulsed to life briefly at the turn of the nineteenth and twentieth centuries, before disappearing off the map.

56   The distance was probably closer to nine miles. Jacob traveled on the Central Ferry Road to the Central Ferry on the Stanislaus River. The road and the crossing appear on *Copperopolis, California, 1916*, U.S.G.S. map #297183 at http://nationalmap.gov/historical/. For background on the Central Ferry, see the "O'Byrnes and Central Ferry" web page at CalaverasHistory.org, https://www.calaverashistory.org/.

57   The distance was probably closer to eight miles. The Howell farm was 160 acres composed of two contiguous parcels: Meridian: Mount Diablo, CA; Township – Range: 001N – 013E [1 North – 13 East], Section 8: S1/2 SW1/4, and Section 17: N1/2 NW1/4, Calaveras County, California. James Howell formally acquired title on July 30, 1873, Document #4918. Source: The Bureau of Land Management, General Land Office records, at https://glorecords.blm.gov/. He paid $200 ($1.25 per acre).

James Howell's 160-acre parcel is now a tiny piece of a 5,000-acre ranch, Loliondo, owned by Dr. James D. Morrissey of Stockton. In 2018 Dr. Morrissey kindly showed me around Loliondo, and, if our calculations were correct, we walked over the Howell family's farm, where Jacob Pike and Mary Howell were married. Nearby, we also walked along the Central Ferry Road, which Jacob traveled on that fateful day when his horse balked.

58   Women were scarce in the Southern Mines, where Jacob was active during his first ten years in California. In 1850 women totaled only 800 (2.7%) versus 30,000

males. Even ten years later, the female population had only grown to 19% (9,000 women versus 50,000 men). Susan Lee Johnson, *Roaring Camp: The Social World of the California Gold Rush* (New York: W. W. Norton & Company, 2000), 280.

HIS HORSE BALKS, HE MEETS MARY
1859, Ages–Jacob 28, Mary 17

59 Jacob's horse had reason to balk. The Stanislaus River was at the bottom of a canyon, and the Central Ferry Road rose abruptly 500 feet in the first half mile after leaving the river, a gradient of almost 20 percent.

60 Could Jacob mistakenly have written "Gastlin's" instead of "Garcelon's"? "The Peach Orchard Farm had been established in the 1850's…on the Old Antelope Trail. The farm was started by [Harris] Garcelon and [Ossian] Kallenback. They planted an orchard and raised vegetables. It was just on the edge of the tree line, of that part of Bear Mountain that must have had better weather for vegetable gardening… perpetual stream of water that came through the farm, from above, from springs on Bear Mountain. They built a two story hotel and made it into a stage stop…" "*Las Calaveras*," Quarterly Bulletin of the Calaveras County Historical Society, Oct. 2005, vol. 54, no. 1, "Memories of the Old Original 'Red House' in Salt Spring Valley" by Ella McCarty Hiatt, 5.

61 Edith Simpson was married to Roy M. Pike, Jacob's son, in 1910, two years before Jacob wrote his memoir. Edith would soon have two children, Roy Jr. in 1913 and Peter in 1914 (my father).

JACOB AND MARY ARE MARRIED
1860, Ages–Jacob 29, Mary 18

62 The Agricultural Schedule to the 1860 U.S. Census documented the Howell farm: Acres of Land: 40 improved land, 400 acres unimproved land (not woodland). Cash Value: $2,000 of farm, $100 of farm implements and machinery, Livestock: 8 horses, 60 milch cows, 8 working oxen, 40 other cattle, 40 swine. Value of all stock: $4,000. No crops of wheat, rye, or Indian corn. Dairy Products: 200 pounds of butter. Hay: 30 tons. U.S. Census 1860, Schedule 4 - Productions of Agriculture, Township 8, County of Calaveras, Post Office Angels Camp, pp. 5–6. Note: James Howell was incorrectly enumerated as "James Harrald."

63 Jacob's wife, Mary Howell, was born Jan. 26, 1842, in Russellville, Arkansas. On the date of their wedding, Jacob was twenty-nine, and Mary was eighteen.

COPPEROPOLIS BOOMS
1861, Ages–Jacob 30, Mary 19

64 Copper was the primary element of brass and bronze, needed by the Union Army to manufacture armaments and munitions.

65 "Two of the first families to establish homes in town were those of Jacob M. Pike and William Kennedy Casement." Rhoda and Charles A. Stone, *The Tools Are on the Bar: The History of Copperopolis, Calaveras County, California* (privately published, 1991), 11.

    Casement makes a brief reference to Copperopolis in his handwritten, twenty-three-page autobiography. See page ten of the typed transcription in the archives of the Society of California Pioneers.

    https://oac.cdlib.org/ark:/13030/kt1w10197f/?order=3&brand=oac4.

66 "Pike and Brothers have a good store." Henry O. Mace, *Between the Rivers: A History of Early Calaveras County*, California, 2nd ed. (Murphys, CA: Paul Groh Press, 2002), 76. The Pike brothers were Jacob, his oldest brother, Sam, and younger brother, William.

67 Four years later, J. M. Pike & Brothers advertised dozens of goods for sale, including "Groceries and Provisions, Hardware and Crockery, Mining Tools and Blasting Powder, Hemp and Manila Rope…Champagne and Wines, Ale and Porter…Assorted Syrups and Bitters, Sarsaparillas and Patent Medicines…Gentlemen's Furnishing Goods…Dusters, Overshirts…White Linen…Shirts and Collars…Ladies, Misses, and Children…Boots, Shoes and Gaiters. Call and examine our stock, not forgetting our motto, 'Light Profits and Quick Returns.'" *Copperopolis Courier*, Jun. 17, 1865, 3.

68 Jacob Pike was appointed the first postmaster of Copperopolis on December 19, 1861.

69 In 1865, a newspaper correspondent raved about Copperopolis: "This community is one of the most flourishing and active towns in the interior of the State—a town

containing twenty-two saloons, three blacksmith shops, six stores, two druggists, three livery stables, two wagon-maker shops, four hotels, three restaurants, three schools, two churches, and a weekly newspaper—a town consisting of good buildings, some of them even elegant, having a population of nearly 2,000." Ronald H. Limbaugh and Willard P. Fuller, *Calaveras Gold: The Impact of Mining on a Mother Lode County* (Reno, NV: University of Nevada Press, 2004), 78.

COPPEROPOLIS BUSTS
1865, Ages–Jacob 34, Mary 23

70 When the Civil War ended, copper fell from an all-time high of 55 cents a pound to 19 cents.

71 "B. C. Horn & Co., importers and jobbers, cigars and tobacco, SW corner of Front & Clay Streets," *San Francisco Directory 1867*, 257.

72 The Pikes first appear living at "Page St near Market St.," *San Francisco City Directory 1867*, 393.

SACRAMENTO TO PORTLAND BY STAGECOACH
1866, Age 35

73 The timetable for the California and Oregon Stage Company listed daily departures from Sacramento to Portland for a fare of $45.00. The distance was 642 miles, and horses would be changed "every twelve miles." Traveling twenty-four hours a day, the trip in the "Spring, Summer and Fall would be 5½ days and in the Winter 10 days." Meals cost an extra 50 to 75 cents. The stagecoach route generally followed later U.S. Route 99, up California's Central Valley to Yreka, over the Siskiyou Pass to Jacksonville, Oregon, and up the Willamette Valley to Portland. *Bancroft's Guide for Travelers by Railway, Stage, and Steam Navigation in the Pacific States* (San Francisco: H. H. Bancroft & Co., Jul. 1869), 84.

SALT LAKE CITY MISSION

74 "Weil & Co., importers and jobbers, cigars and tobacco, 226 Front, and proprietors Vuelta Abajo Havana Cigar Factory, 34 California," *San Francisco Directory 1867*, 491.

FINDING BROTHER GEORGE

75 George Pike was killed in 1883, when he was the engineer for a construction train on the Northern Pacific Line. "The train was running [east] about forty miles an hour, and as they were rounding a sharp curve near the Elk Creek bridge, a gravel train was sighted running west…as they met, the tender of the gravel train jumped fairly on top of Pike's engine, crushing Pike…" *The Railway Age*, vol. 8, Jul. 26, 1883, 450.

76 Jacob mistakenly wrote "Vancouver, Oregon."

BRIGHAM YOUNG'S BALL
1870, Age 39

77 "We take pleasure in noting the arrival in this city of a party of gentlemen representing the leading business houses…in San Francisco…San Francisco has, strangely enough, not made the efforts to secure the trade of this region which have been made by Eastern cities. Yet she possesses great advantages…" Among the dozen members of the trade delegation was "J. M. Pike, Esq., of Weil & Co., importers and manufacturers of tobacco and cigars," "San Franciscans at Salt Lake," *Daily Alta California*, Jul. 13, 1870, 1, reprinted from the *Salt Lake Herald* of Jul. 1, 1870.

NEW YORK BAKERY AND RESTAURANT

78 New York Bakery, Baldwin, Pike & Bertz proprietors, 626 and 628 Kearny, *San Francisco City Directory 1872*, 494, and Jacob M. Pike *(Baldwin, P. & Bertz)*, dwl 631 Sacramento, *San Francisco City Directory 1872*, 529.

79 Baldwin, Pike & Bertz *(O. D. Baldwin, Jacob M. Pike, and Jacob Bertz)* proprietors New York Bakery and restaurant, 626 and 628 Kearny, *San Francisco City Directory 1872*, 82, and O. D. Baldwin (Baldwin & Pike) res Napa, *San Francisco City Directory 1872*, 82.

80 New York Bakery, Jacob M. Pike proprietor, 626 and 628 Kearny, *San Francisco City Directory 1874*, 499, and Jacob M. Pike proprietor, New York Bakery, 626 and 628 Kearny, dwl 414 Tyler, *San Francisco City Directory 1874*, 536. Tyler Street was renamed Golden Gate Avenue after the completion of Golden Gate Park.

UNITED STATES RESTAURANT
1873, Age 42

81 United States Restaurant, Jacob M. Pike, proprietor, 548 Clay, *San Francisco City Directory 1875*, 723, and Jacob M. Pike, proprietor, United States Restaurant, 548 Clay, and New York Bakery, 626 and 628 Kearny, dwl 414 Tyler, *San Francisco City Directory 1875*, 595.

82 "Perhaps the most popular… [restaurant] patronized by all classes—rich as well as poor—is the United States Restaurant. The prices charged at this restaurant are presumably as low as good wholesome food can be furnished. One dish for fifteen cents, or three for twenty-five cents. Of course, when extras are desired, a price in proportion to the rareness of the dish is had. For ordinary food, however, the above popular prices are maintained.

"It would be a matter of wonder and surprise to anyone unacquainted with the eating habits of San Franciscans, to spend a day inside this restaurant and observe the great number of persons that it feeds. A fair estimate of the number of meals served per diem at this one eating house would place the daily average at three thousand. The average daily receipts are $600, which would make the average price per meal twenty cents." Benjamin E. Lloyd, *Lights and Shades in San Francisco* (San Francisco: A. L. Bancroft, 1876), 64.

83 J. M. Pike & Co. (Thomas Dowling and George W. Downey), importers and wholesale grocers, 125 and 127 California, *San Francisco City Directory 1876*, 656, and Jacob M. Pike proprietor United States Restaurant, 548 Clay, and New York Bakery, 626 Kearny *(and J. M. Pike & Co.)*, dwl 414 Tyler, *San Francisco City Directory 1876*, 656.

CROSS-COUNTRY CENTENNIAL TRIP
1876, Ages–Jacob 45, Mary 34

84 Charles W. Pike was born in Copperopolis on Nov. 13, 1861.

85 Laura Celia Pike was born in Copperopolis on July 14, 1863.

86 Centennial International Exposition in Philadelphia.

87 "We had the pleasure of meeting Mr. Pike, of California, in our little city last Tuesday. Mr. Pike and family are kinsman of the clever Geo. Howell. They reside in the far western Golden State, and will visit Philadelphia, taking in the big show and other big cities and other watering places, before they return to California." *Russellville Democrat*, May 18, 1876, 4.

88 "Mr. Jacob Pike and family of San Francisco, formerly residents of Eastport, are visiting their relatives here." *Eastport Sentinel*, Jun. 21, 1876, 2.

89 His mother, who had remarried after her husband's death, was again a widow, Lydia Cutter Pike Mathews.

90 His married sister was Celia Paine.

91 On July 10, the *Philadelphia Enquirer* headlined: "One Hundred and Four in the Shade, Numerous Deaths in the City." For the past twenty-two days "the mercury has not gone below 80°, while the average has been somewhere about 95°." *Philadelphia Enquirer*, Jul. 10, 1876, 4.

FINANCIAL PANIC STRIKES SAN FRANCISCO
1877, Age 46

92 When the Consolidated Virginia Mines of the Comstock Lode could not pay its normal monthly dividend in January 1877, "A panic in mining stocks resulted, with prices tumbling headlong to the lowest recorded levels." Ira B. Cross, *Financing an Empire: History of Banking in California*, vol. 1. (Chicago: S. J. Clarke Publishing Co., 1927), 370.

CIGAR FACTORY FAILS
1881, Age 50

93 J. M. Pike & Son (Jacob M. and Charles W.) manufacturers cigars, 324 Battery, *San Francisco City Directory 1882*, 775. Charles W. Pike (J. M. Pike & Son) r 414 Golden Gate Av, *San Francisco City Directory 1882*, 775. Jacob M. Pike (J. M. Pike & Son) r 414 Golden Gate Av, *San Francisco City Directory 1882*, 775.

JACOB BUYS ANOTHER RESTAURANT

94 Swain's Bakery and Restaurant, Jacob M. Pike proprietor, 636 Market, *San Francisco City Directory 1887*, 1134. Jacob M. Pike, proprietor Swain's Bakery and Restaurant, 636 Market (and J. M. Pike & Co.) r 414 Golden Gate Av, *San Francisco City Directory 1887*, 961. Pike J. M. & Co. (Jacob M. Pike, Edward S. Pond and William J. Smith) manufacturers cigars, 324 Battery, *San Francisco City Directory 1887*, 961.

95 Manning's Restaurant and Oyster Grotto, J. M. Pike & Co. proprietors, *oysters in every style, apartments for ladies and their escorts, oysters delivered to all parts of the city* [italics original], 13–15 Powell, *San Francisco City Directory 1892*, 907. Baldwin House [hotel], Holm & Saxtorph proprietors, 14–16 Ellis, *San Francisco City Directory 1892*, 208. J. M. Pike & Co. (J. M. Pike and J. J. Cook) proprietors Manning's Restaurant and Oyster Grotto, 13–15 Powell, *San Francisco City Directory 1892*, 1118. J. M. Pike (J. M. Pike & Co.) r. 1406 Webster, *San Francisco City Directory 1892*, 1118.

MARY DIES
1892, Ages–Jacob 61, Mary 50

96 Mary Howell Pike's handwritten will remains in the possession of the family. This is a transcription:

"Realizing the uncertainty of life, I, Mary L. Pike, make this my last Will & Testament: To J. M. Pike, my husband, all money I have in the Peoples Home Savings Bank and in the German Savings Bank. To my eldest son, Charles W. Pike, one diamond stone to be made by him into a ring. To my well-beloved daughter, Laura Pike Fuller, my cluster diamond ring. To Willis Pike, my second son, my solitaire diamond ring. Also, to my 3 other sons, namely Thomas H., Roy M., and Percy M. Pike, I bequeath each a stone to be given to each said son when he is

18 years of age. I request the smaller stones be sold & a solitaire bought for Percy M. Pike by his father. I also add that at the death of my husband, J. M. Pike, that his Life Insurance Policy made in my name I favor be divided share & share alike between my four youngest boys, namely Willis Pike, Thomas H. Pike, Roy M. Pike and Percy M. Pike. My reason for this is my older children are well provided for. I wish to appoint my husband to be executor without bonds."

(signed) Mary L. Pike

November 17th, 1890

97   Jacob's youngest son, Percy, vividly recalled her death. "On her death bed, older brother Charles promised Mother he would take care of Roy (then fourteen), and sister Laura promised she would take care of me (then ten years of age), and Mother, relieved, turned over and died. Home was broken up and Father stored the furniture." Jacob M. Pike and Percy M. Pike, *Memoirs of J. M. Pike and Percy Mortimer Pike* (Los Angeles: Privately printed, 1968), 42.

YOSEMITE INNKEEPER

98   John J. ("J.J.") Cook was Jacob's partner in Manning's Restaurant. John J. Cook (J. M. Pike & Co.) r. Yosemite, Mariposa Co., *San Francisco City Directory 1893*, 392. Manning's Restaurant and Oyster Grotto, J. M. Pike & Co. proprietors, *oysters in every style, apartments for ladies and their escorts, oysters delivered to all parts of the city* [italics original], 13–15 Powell, *San Francisco City Directory 1893*, 924. J. M. Pike & Co. (J. M. Pike and J. J. Cook) proprietors Manning's Restaurant and Oyster Grotto, 13-15 Powell, *San Francisco City Directory 1893*, 1140. J. M. Pike (J. M. Pike & Co.) r. 136 McAllister, *San Francisco City Directory 1893*, 1140.

99   The hotel was Stoneman House, operated by J.J. Cook for the State of California. It was located adjacent to today's Stoneman Meadow. "In 1885 $40,000 was appropriated [by the state] to build a modern, first-class hotel to accommodate 150 guests. Muir, for one, thought the finished, four-story structure, bulking in the shadow of Glacier Point, had 'a silly look amidst surrounds so massive and sublime.' Since George Stoneman was governor then, the huge inn became the Stoneman House, and the nearby meadow became Stoneman Meadow." Shirley Sargent, *Yosemite's Innkeepers: The Story of a Great Park and Its Chief Concessionaires*

(Yosemite: Ponderosa Press, 2000), 4. See also Hank Johnston, *The Yosemite Grant, 1864–1906: A Pictorial History* (Yosemite National Park, CA: Yosemite Association, 1995), 146, 153–57, and 205–06 (pictures of Stoneman House on page 154).

Stoneman House burned down in 1896. "Yosemite, Aug. 24—At 2 o'clock this morning the Stoneman House, together with its entire contents, was burned to the ground… It was beautifully situated, directly under Glacier Point and at the end of the stage road. From the verandas of the Stoneman tourists could view Eagle Peak, Yosemite Falls, Royal Arches, North Dome, Cloud's Rest, Half Dome and Grizzly, Moran and Glacier Points. The Stoneman was a large and commodious building, and with its charming location and excellent accommodations, was a favorite resort for visitors to the valley… J.J. Cook has conducted the hotel for a number of years." *Sacramento Daily Union*, Aug. 25, 1896, 8.

"At about two o'clock last Monday morning the Stoneman House in Yosemite Valley was discovered on fire… At the time of the fire the only occupants were J.J. Cook, the proprietor, Doc Lincoln and wife, L. F. Starks, the clerk, and two guests, Miss Becht of San Francisco and Miss Fannie Bruce of Wawona… The building was a State institution and was rented to J.J. Cook at a yearly rental of $1,200." *Mariposa Gazette*, Aug. 29, 1896, 1.

TYNAN HOTEL, MODESTO
1895–1911, Age 64–80

100 Built by Dr. Thomas Tynan, the Tynan Hotel opened in 1890. It was a three-story building located at the northwest corner of 10th and H Streets in Modesto. Although the structure included a Victorian clock tower, no clock was ever installed. "Despite its timekeeping deficiencies, the Tynan was the finest of the town's hotels during this period, with its rooms priced at 50 cents, 75 cents, and $1 per night. It reportedly provided the first elevator service in the San Joaquin Valley and had a speaking tube that connected each room to the lobby desk. The Tynan also had a 12-foot ceiling, spacious arched halls, marble fireplaces, ornate gas lighting fixtures, and original oil paintings (some depicting Yosemite scenes)." Colleen Stanley Bare, *Modesto Then and Now* (Modesto: McHenry Museum Press, 1999), 38–39. Picture of the Tynan Hotel on pages 68–69. Later known as the State Hotel, the building was demolished in 1961.

101 Located on Front Street near I Street, Ross House opened in 1871. It burned down in 1897. Colleen Stanley Bare, *Modesto Then and Now* (Modesto: McHenry Museum Press, 1999), 34.

102 In recognition of Jacob Pike's affection for Modesto, his youngest son Percy bought seven acres of land that he deeded to the City of Modesto for a park at 1601 Princeton Ave. (at the northwestern corner of Kearney Ave.). City of Modesto Resolution #7988, Jul. 21, 1948. Today it is known as the J. M. Pike Park.

JACOB PREPARES HIS WILL

103 After Jacob and Charles Pike dissolved their cigar manufacturing partnership, Charles apparently did well financially as a "shipping and commission merchant" per the *San Francisco City Directory*. However, he disappeared under mysterious circumstances in 1928. "Man Missing in Bank Fraud Feared Dead, Son Tells Police $300,000 Vanished Under Mystic Spell of Aide... Robert D. Pike... son of Charles W. Pike... believes [his father] will not be found alive... The son blamed his father's difficulties and loss of a fortune of $300,000 on Philip Hackett... He believed Hackett was possessed of a certain strange spiritualistic influence." *San Francisco Chronicle*, Sep. 14, 1928, 9.

104 Laura Celia Pike had married William Parmer Fuller, the owner of W. P. Fuller & Company, a paint manufacturing company, in 1887.

OTHER WRITINGS

Chased by a Bear, 1850

Handwritten by Jacob M. Pike, 1912

In 1850, when Sam[1] and myself were working on Roger's Bar on the Tuolumne River.

On one Sunday morning, Sam told me he would take his gun and go out to kill enough quail for dinner. He started out and had been gone for about half an hour. I looked out of the tent door and see Sam running toward the tent as though the d__l [devil[2]] was after him. As he came near, I noticed his eyes were as big as small saucers. I said to him, "For God's sake, Sam, what is the matter?"

He was so exhausted he could not speak for a few seconds. When he got his breath, he said he was chased by a brown bear with three cubs. It seemed he came on the bear and three cubs very suddenly, and, as soon as the bear saw "Sam," she thought he was after her cubs. And she put after Sam at full tilt. She ran after him and, all at once, she stopped and returned to her cubs.

That is the nature of bears, not to get very far away from her cubs. A very lucky thing for Sam. For when she turned to go back, she was only ten feet away from him. But he never stopped running until he got home. And a more frightened man, you never saw. If the bear had kept after him a few seconds more, she would have caught him.

I don't blame him for being frightened after so close a race for his life. Thanks to the cubs that were left behind, that was the only thing that saved him. I never remember him going quail shooting after that bear experience.

Brown bears are never very vicious and do not attack anyone if they do not have cubs. The result was we ate our dinner minus quail. After it was all over, we had a good deal of fun out of Sam by being run home by a brown bear. [underline original]

---

1   Samuel Tuttle Pike was Jacob's oldest brother (b. 1826, d. 1915).

2   Apparently, Jacob thought it impolite to write out the word "devil."

Shooting a Grizzly Bear, 1853

Handwritten by Jacob M. Pike, 1912

When we were working on Morgan's Bar, Tuolumne River, I think it was 1853.

My brother Sam, myself, and three others were in our tent at noon eating lunch. A man came rushing in very much excited, saying there was a large bear right at the top of a steep hill nearby our tent. And he seemed to be asleep under a large acorn tree. We jumped up and took three rifles, all of which were heavily loaded.

We immediately started up the hill, pulled by the man that gave us the information. The hill was very steep. We walked very slowly and made no noise for we wanted to get within gun shot of the bear without interfering with his slumber. We finally got to the top of the hill and could see the bear through some brush, and it was still sleeping.

We held a consultation as to how to make the attack. We were about two hundred yards away. We concluded to get up closer, if we possibly could. So we agreed to creep on our hands and knees, at least the three of us that had the rifles, and not to speak above a whisper and avoid breaking brush.

We got along nicely within about seventy-five yards of the bear and stopped. We agreed to shoot all at once and to aim at the fore shoulder (a fatal spot). We took aim and fired. When the smoke cleared away, we noticed he had turned a little over on one side and was a dead bear. We examined him and found our three shots had hit him in the fore shoulder where we intended that they should go. He was the largest grizzly bear I ever saw up to that time or since.

Now the question was how we could get the dead bear to the camp. We sent a man down to the store we traded at to borrow a long, stout rope and get more men to help us. It was very lucky for us that the hill was steep and the dead bear was right at the top of it.

We had no scales to weigh him, but everyone said he weighed between eight hundred and nine hundred pounds. He surely was a monster.

The man came back with the rope and with five men to help pull it down the hill. We tied the rope around the bear's neck. It took us some time to start him, but when we got him started down the steep hill, he went to the bottom mighty quick. We cut his four paws off. His claws were about five inches long and sharp as needles. If he had ever got hold of a man, he would have made mincemeat of him in short order.

Then we skinned him. It made an immense bear robe. Next morning, we cut him up and all on the [river] bar had all the bear meat they wanted. However, they got sick of it very soon. It was tough as tripe. I had one mess of it; that was enough for me. He had seen a great many summers. He was what you might call an old ranger.

The only thing I regret is that I did not keep one of his paws and the bear robe as souvenirs.

Mining With the Hatheway Brothers, 1854

Handwritten by Jacob M. Pike, 1912

In my former memories, I was speaking about meeting my old friend and schoolmate [Charlie Hatheway[1]] on the trail going up the Tuolumne River. He was then working on Indian Bar about five miles up the river from where I was working on Morgan's Bar. After that, we were together a great deal. After I went to the Stanislaus River in 1854, I sent for Charlie[2] to come to the Stanislaus River to work with me on a claim that I had located on Nasty Bar, just above my claim on Grand Bar that I had located when I first went over to the Stanislaus River.

After we got to work on the mine, Charlie sent home for his brother Henry[3] to come to California to work in the mine with him. In due course, Henry arrived at the mine. I do not think he had ever done a day's work in his life. He was dressed up and looked like a country jumper more than he looked like a miner. I asked him if he had any old clothes. He said he had. "Well, you put them on in the morning, and we will try to make a miner out of you."

I will never forget the expression on his countenance when he looked over the bank and saw where he had to work. He had to shovel into the sluice boxes eight feet high and every shovel full of dirt he would throw into the sluice boxes would splash muddy water all over his shoulders. Of course, we pitied the poor fellow, and all made it as easy for him as we possibly could.

The first day's work was a hard one on Henry. When we quit work, his hands were badly blistered. After we had supper, we doctored his hands up, and he went to bed (not a very soft bed either) a tired boy. When he got up in the morning, his hands were pretty sore. He went to work rather reluctantly. But after he worked a while, he felt better. He soon got hardened up to the work and was all right.

We surely had lots of fun with him breaking him in. I never laughed so much in my life as I did with poor Henry. It's a fact that he wished himself back to old Eastport many a time. But we were making money, and that was an incentive. We struck a pocket in the bed rock one day and took out $200 in one pan of dirt. That was encouraging for Henry, and he worked along like a good fellow after that but always said he was not cut out for a miner and would not work at it long.

The mine at Nasty Bar was worked out in 1861 or 1862. Charlie & Henry came to Copperopolis. Charlie went to work for the Union Copper Mine, and Henry enlisted in the Union Army and went to Texas. His company got into a fight with Indians, and he was shot in the right wrist and his right hand was disabled for life as the bullet cut the cords of his hand. At the close of the Civil War, he was honorably discharged. And now he is drawing a pension from the Government. He is living now in Houlton, Maine, with ample means to live on.[4] After the War closed, he married an Eastport girl of a fine family. She died, I think, about 20 years ago. They had no children.

Charlie married in Copperopolis. His wife was from Calais, Maine. They had two children. Charlie is living with his daughter Mrs. Brann[5] in Oakland. His wife died about two years ago.

---

1   Charles Daniel Hatheway (b. 1834, Eastport, Maine, d. unk).

2   Jacob spelled Charles Hatheway's first name as "Charlie." In a letter to Jacob from Henry Hatheway in 1892, he spelled his brother's name "Charley." I have transcribed the name as Jacob wrote it.

3   Henry P. Hatheway (b. 1835, Eastport, Maine, d. unk).

4   After Jacob's wife, Mary, died in 1892, Henry wrote to him: "She was associated with the pleasures of my early manhood and did, in a measure, unconsciously influence my acts for good, for which I have always revered and respected her." Letter from Henry Hatheway to Jacob Pike, Houlton, Maine, May 10, 1892.

5   Charlie Hatheway's daughter, Jessie Benton Hatheway, married Walter Scott Brann, Apr. 15, 1903. Source: Franklin Harper, ed., *Who's Who on the Pacific Coast: A Biographical Compilation of Notable Living Contemporaries West of the Rocky Mountains* (Los Angeles: Harper Publishing Company, 1913), 66. https://hdl.handle.net/2027/loc.ark:/13960/t4mk73d70.

Trip to Yosemite Valley in the Spring of 1857

Handwritten by Jacob M. Pike, 1912

We made a party of fourteen persons, two of whom were ladies, wives of two of the gentlemen in our party.[1]

There were no wagon roads into the Valley at that time. Had to go in on an Indian trail.[2] Rode in on horseback and packed our provisions and camping outfit on mules. Just before this time there was some trouble with Indians in the Valley. They killed two white men. Under those circumstances we all armed ourselves for any emergency that might occur.

The distance to the Valley from where we started at the mill[3] was about seventy-five miles. We arrived in the Valley three days from the time we started. Met a great many Indians,[4] but all were friendly. We being so well armed was a good conciliator. We treated them right, and they were a good help to us while in the Valley. Such as making trails and catching trout for our camp. You bet we lived high, as trout of the finest quality were in abundance there in all the streams.

We struck camp on the banks of the Merced River. The river runs right through the center of the Valley. That being springtime, the Valley was in its beauty. A grander sight no one ever beheld. Of course, it was harder to get around then as now, for now there are fine trails to all points of interest which have been built by the government.[5] At the time we were there, there were no trails or facilities to get anywhere if you did not make them with your feet.

Vernal Fall[6] was located a short distance from our camp, and, at that time of the year, there was a large quantity of water coming over it. At our camp all were anxious to go to the top of Vernal Fall, including the two women. So we concluded to give it a trial next day, which we did. But only three of us and the two ladies would attempt it. We put up our lunch and started for our conquest.

We got up to the bottom of the fall, as far from the water to one side as we could. I forgot to mention that we took our pack rope with us for fear we might need it. We examined the fall pretty thoroughly and concluded we had a very dangerous proposition before us. However we tackled it, the distance we had to climb to the top was about fifty feet. We selected the most secure spot and started. What we had to climb was nearly perpendicular.

We had made arrangements with the two ladies. If we got up safe, they could climb up as far as possible. We would take our rope with us and lower it down to them. They would tie it around them under their arms, and we would pull them up. They said all right, they would do it. They were as anxious to get on top of the falls as we were.

It took us some time to get up. Oh, it was so dangerous. Never could have accomplished it were it not for some strong brush growing out of the crevices of the rock. The ladies had climbed up about twenty feet and could not climb any further. When they see we were up all right, they commenced to holler for us to lower the rope and heave them up.

We did as they commanded and pulled them up one at a time. Not the worse for wear, but a little disfigured in the way of torn dresses. After that experience they were the heroes of the whole party. Surely, they displayed nerve that you seldom see in ladies.

Right at the top of these falls is a large basin, some 50-feet wide by 75-feet long.[7] The basin is cut out by the water in solid granite rock and the pure water cold and clear as crystal. Right there we set down and took our lunch. We were as hungry as bears after the great experience we had in climbing the fall. We were the only party that ever did that.

One party, Mr. Campi, proprietor of Campi's Restaurant of San Francisco, tried to climb Vernal Fall sometime after that.[8] He fell and was killed instantly. I was well acquainted with him. Right after his death, the government built good substantial steps over the falls.[9] The scenery at the top of the falls and the pretty granite basin formed there by the continual action of the water was a sight well worth the risking of your life to see it.

Now the question was how we were to get back. Our rope was of no use to get back. We finally concluded to take a long way around the falls and make it that way if possible. It was worse for the ladies than the men. We started on our journey for home. We finally made camp, and you ought to have seen us. We were the most pitiful looking group you ever saw, our clothes torn in threads by climbing over rock and through bushes. A rougher country that no one ever traveled through.

One of the ladies that was with us, her name was Mrs. Coulter.[10] Her husband located the Town of Coulterville in the early part of 1850.[11] At that time, it was a prominent mining town. The other lady I have been racking my brain to remember her name, but for the life of me I cannot. So I will have to let it go at that. At all events she was a good, a true blue. She was full of life and as brave and nervy as a lion. It was even so with Mrs. Coulter. Surely, they both were heroes and proved themselves in scaling Vernal Fall, a feat that never had been accomplished before nor since by either man or woman.

When we arrived in Camp, they had our supper all ready, and it is enough to say we enjoyed it perfectly for rest assured we were hungry and tired from our day's trample and experience. The wondrous scenery offset such dangers we had to go through to see it.

We were in the Valley three weeks. As said before, we made friends with the Indians of which there was a large number, and they seemed to regret that we were going to leave. A few days after we went to Vernal Fall we packed up and started for home.

On leaving the Valley we had to go up a mountain which was about four miles long. Having been in the valley three weeks, we did not use our horses and mules much. The wild feed was so heavy that our stock got rolling fat and seemed to enjoy having something to do. So the four-mile hill was just what they wanted. We got up to the top of the hill and took a rest and a drink of the pure Yosemite cold water, which was more than refreshing.

We started again. Myself and one of our company were ahead on the trail. We were riding along leisurely. We came on to a top of a rise in the trail, and there was a big grizzly bear lying right across the trail in front of us. He gave a snort soon as he seen us and ran into the thick bush nearby. We followed him up to the brush, but we did not follow him into the brush. We thought best not to take any chances on Mr. Grizzly, so we let him go. We both had rifles but could not get a shot at him before he got to the brush.

Without any further incident, we all arrived home fat, happy in the prime of health, and more than satisfied with our Yosemite Valley trip. This is the eighth sheet which is much more than I thought it would be to tell the story. But if it is interesting to you and Edith, I am glad it is long.[12]

---

1   The party was led by George W. Coulter, the founder of Coulterville.

2   Coulter had blazed a trail into Yosemite Valley the previous year in 1856. See Hank Johnston, ed., *Ho! For Yo-Semite: By Foot, Horseback, Horse-Stage, Horseless Carriage, Bicycle, & Steam Locomotive* (El Portal, CA: Yosemite Association, 2000), 4, and Linda W. Greene, *Yosemite the Park and Its Resources: Historic Resource Study* (National Park Service, 1987), 32, 42, 78. http://www.yosemite.ca.us/library/yosemite_resources/yosemite_resources.pdf.

3   Jacob probably started from the sawmill near Coulterville, mentioned in his memoir under the section "Jacob's Sawmill Venture Fails." See a map of the Coulterville Trail and Coulterville Road in Hank Johnston, *The Yosemite Grant, 1864–1906: A Pictorial History* (Yosemite National Park, CA: Yosemite Association, 1995), 126–27. To trace an approximation of this route today, see *Northern California Atlas & Gazetteer* (Yarmouth, Maine: DeLorme, 2000, Fifth Edition), 109–110. Leaving Coulterville, follow (roughly) Greely Hill Road (J132), Jordan Creek Road, Briceburg Road, Old Yosemite Road (State Route 2S01), and Old Coulterville Road (Forest Route 1S12 / Tuolumne River Road / Forest Route 2S84).

4   For historical background, see the National Park Service document, *Historic Resources of Yosemite Park*, Jun. 2, 2014, 12–13. https://www.nps.gov/nr/feature/places/pdfs/64501214.pdf See also Linda W. Greene, *Yosemite the Park and Its Resources: Historic Resource Study* (National Park Service, 1987), 56–61. https://www.yosemite.ca.us/library/yosemite_resources/.

5   Jacob wrote this account in 1912.

6   Jacob mis-identified the waterfall as Nevada Fall in his handwritten account, but it was certainly Vernal Fall, which lies below Nevada Fall.

7   Emerald Pool is a small, shallow lake located immediately above Vernal Fall.

8   Giacomo Campi fell to his death on March 28, 1871. See Michael P. Ghiglieri and Charles R. Farabee Jr., *Off the Wall: Death in Yosemite* (Flagstaff, AZ: Puma Press, Third Revision, 2007), 184. "While climbing a rickety ladder beside Vernal Fall, Campi, a restaurateur in San Francisco, stopped to offer assistance to a lady. She declined his hand. He stepped back to bow graciously but stepped into empty air and fell 35 feet to fracture his skull."

9   See Hank Johnston, "Yosemite's Vernal Falls Ladders," *Sierra Heritage*, April 2013. See also pictures of the old ladders in Hank Johnston, *The Yosemite Grant, 1864–1906: A Pictorial History* (Yosemite National Park, CA: Yosemite Association, 1995), 102–103. See also James Mason Hutchings, *Scenes of Wonder and Curiosity in California* (San Francisco: J. M. Hutchings & Co., 1862), 112–114. See https://archive.org/details/sceneswonderando01hutcgoog. See also, "Nevada Fall Corridor: A Cultural Landscape Report," a thesis, Interdisciplinary Studies Program: Historic Preservation, University of Oregon, Aug. 2004, 11, 20, 23. https://scholarsbank.uoregon.edu/xmlui/handle/1794/3937.

10 Margaret Backhouse Coulter (b. 1817, d. 1891)

11 George Wilson Coulter. (b. 1818, d. 1902)

12 Edith Simpson had married Roy Pike in 1910.

Drumming Trip to Washington Territory, 1878

Through Northern Oregon and Washington Territory [W.T.],
Now State of Washington
Handwritten by Jacob M. Pike, 1912

In the winter of 1878, I started from San Francisco for Portland, Ore. After drumming Portland, I went to Drain, W.T.[1] Soon as I arrived there, a snowstorm commenced, and I was snow bound there for ten days. The town was cut off from communication and the only way we could get out was by sleigh.

There were four drummers of us, and we clubbed together and hired two sleigh teams to take us to Colfax, W.T., a distance of about twenty miles. Had no idea then, but we could make the train at Colfax for Spokane Falls, our next stopping place.[2]

It had ceased snowing. We ordered the sleighs and started for Colfax over an almost impassible road. We encountered nothing but snowbanks. We were upset three times each and thrown into the snow. Finally, we reached Colfax about sundown, all of us wet and almost freezing from being thrown in the snow so often. We put up at the hotel and, as good luck would have it, they had a fine hot fireplace fire, and we all soon got warm. When we were in condition to enquire what time the train left, we were told on account of the heavy storm they had no train for several days. That was another damper on us, and right there we used lots of curse words. Now we could get no information at what time the train would be through.

The only recourse we had was to get to the Snake River and take the river steamer there for Wallula[3] where we could get railroad accommodations.

Bright and early next morning we got up and hired a four-horse team to take the baggage and ourselves over to the Snake River, a distance of about twelve miles.[4]

The teamster came up to the hotel. The first thing I noticed he had a common old dead-ex wagon which would kill a man to ride on—a dead-ex wagon is a wagon without springs. I asked him if he did not have a wagon with springs. He said No. There was not a four-horse spring wagon in town. I says, May the Lord bless us, and we took the old wagon.

When we got to the Snake River we were a pretty sore crowd, but not as sore as we were when we found that the Snake River steamer would not be there for several days. The River during the storm was very high, and the steamboat met with a mishap and was laid up for repairs. We said surely that was a country for holdups. We had been held up by snow, then by railroad, and now by the steamboat. We considered that pretty hard luck.

Next thing was, How could we get out of this Godforsaken place? There was no hotel there, and, not having any place to sleep or eat, it was either starve or get out of there. By making enquiries we heard of a man that owned a small Gasoline launch (Roy Pike correction: Must have been steam. Gas engines not invented by then).

We rustled around and found him. He asked how many of us. We told him four and baggage. He said my launch is small. If not too much baggage, it's all right. I will take you. So he brought his launch up. We piled in the baggage, and, when we all got in, her deck was only out of water about five inches. The owner said, at the high stage of the river and the swift current, the boat is too deeply loaded. We added a little more to what we were to give him for the trip and he finally agreed to start.

We were very glad for it was getting late, and night would overtake us before getting to our destination. Our own pilot understood the river very well. We were going along finally at a fast pace and making a short turn around a sharp point in the river and only missed it by about ten inches.

At the rate we were going, if we had struck the point in the river, it would have been goodbye to us all because the boat would have upset and dumped us in the river. The current was so swift we never could have got out of the river alive. It was quite dark. From that time on the pilot only kept steerage way on the boat and let the current take us along.

We arrived at Wallula about ten o'clock in the evening. In all of my experiences in traveling that was the most dangerous I ever took. Had we not had a man who understood the Snake River and a launch so well, we surely could never have made it.

We stopped all night at Wallula. Next morning, we took the train for Spokane Falls. Arrived there about noon. It was very cold, down to zero. Did some business in the afternoon. We made arrangements with a livery man to take us out to Lake Coeur d'Alene in two sleighs in the morning early.

We got up early in the morning, and I had to break ice an inch thick in my wash pitcher. That was what you may call cold weather. We took breakfast, ordered the sleighs up at that time. I enquired how cold it was. The proprietor of the hotel told me it was 32 degrees below zero.

The next thing was to bundle up to keep from freezing while we rode over to Lake Coeur d'Alene. We bought a lot of neck comforters for our neck, head, and face and with all the sleigh robes we could get. With all that we rode over to the lake in good condition. Did not even freeze our ears. The weather at noon moderated so we could go without freezing our ears.

We returned to Spokane Falls for dinner. Stayed all night in Spokane Falls and next day. It is a big City, and it took us some time to do our business. From Spokane Falls we went to Walla Walla. Our party separated there.

I went from Walla Walla to The Dalles on the Columbia River and from there to Portland. From Portland to San Francisco to home.

I never was so glad to get home as I was at that time. For my whole trip was continually made thorough danger and hardship of the worst sort.

I did a very fair business, but the profits did not pay me for the risk of life and hardships that I experienced on that Oregon and Washington trip. I can only look back upon it with a shudder.

---

1. Jacob wrote "Drain, W.T." But clearly this was a mistake. Maybe he was confusing the city with Drain, Oregon, which is 500 miles away. Perhaps he should have written Lewiston, W.T., which was roughly twenty miles south of Colfax. (Today, Lewiston is in the state of Idaho on the border with Washington.)
2. Spokane Falls became Spokane in 1891.
3. Wallula, Washington, is on the east side of the Columbia River, just south of the junction of the Snake and Columbia Rivers.
4. Jacob and his party probably went to the town of Amota, the closest point of the Snake River south of Colfax.

APPENDIX

NEWSPAPER ACCOUNTS OF THE SHOOTOUT ON THE STANISLAUS RIVER, 1858

San Joaquin Republican (Stockton), Aug. 7, 1858, p. 2.

DREADFUL AFFRAY ON THE STANISLAUS! — TWO MEN KILLED AND TWO MORTALLY WOUNDED BY FRENCHMEN—PURSUIT OF ASSAILANTS

We are indebted to a friend at Knight's Ferry for the following account of a shooting affair at a point on the Stanislaus, one half way between Central Ferry and Peoria Bar.

Editor Republican: —On the morning of the 4th inst.* a difficulty occurred between some miners on the Stanislaus River near Central Ferry, which resulted in the killing of one man, and the wounding of two others, one of whom, it is supposed, fatally.

It appears that a company of miners was working a bar claim by means of a wheel used for raising water, for sluicing. A company of Frenchmen set in to work just below them with a view of fluming the river, and were engaged in constructing a dam, which they had raised to such a height as to back the water on claims above, stopping the wheels.

This caused a remonstrance from the party on the bar claim. Angry words followed, when the Frenchmen, who were encamped near their claim, repaired to their cabin, seized their double-barreled shot guns, and commenced firing on the unarmed miners, resulting as above stated. Leonard Shoccob was instantly killed; Abram Delay, mortally wounded, Geo Crooks, shot through both thighs.

The Frenchmen made good their escape. A large party are in pursuit.

In addition to the above, we learn from some young men who arrived in town yesterday, that the affair took place at 8 A.M. After the men were

---

* 4th of the current month.

shot a party of miners headed by Mr. Jacob Pike, who kept a store at Peoria, started in pursuit of the Frenchmen, three of whom were involved in the killing.

One of the three had been a soldier and is said to be a deadly sure shot at sixty paces. The fugitives were pursued over the Stanislaus into Tuolumne County, to Short Crop Bar, (two miles) and from thence up to Chaparral Mountain, which is in the same county.

Here the pursued turned and commenced firing on the pursuers. Mr. Pike was instantly killed at the first fire, and Mr. Chas. McKenny mortally wounded. The Frenchmen then continued their flight, and were last seen at the Mountain Saw Mill, two and a half miles from Sonora.

The alarm was given in every direction, and Mr. Robert McMullen, Marshal of Columbia, Mr. Carden, and three other gentlemen, were promptly on the trail. A party also started from Sonora after the desperate fugitives. It is said that they cannot escape.

Peoria Bar is some forty or fifty miles from this city. The Frenchmen had some twenty Chinamen employed on their work. Those remaining are much alarmed, as great excitement prevails. Mr. Pike has a brother in this city, one in Montezuma, and one a teamster on the road. He was about twenty-six years of age. The man first killed was a German.

Since the above was written, we learn that Sheriff O'Neal, of this city, received a letter from Knight's Ferry, requesting him to intercept the fugitives should they attempt escape by way of the San Francisco steamer.

They are described as "brothers and about thirty-five years of age. One is a very large, muscular man, heavy jaws, mustache and imperial; had on a pair of dirty canvas pants, a grey or white undershirt, and a Panama hat. The other was somewhat smaller, but a stout built man, dark complexion, with a face covered with heavy black hair; had on a pair of blue overalls, blue shirt, and a low crowned black felt hat. Both had double barreled guns, powder flask, shot belt, game bag, pistol and knife. A dog accompanied them when they left."

The Sheriff did not succeed in finding any trace of them.

Daily Alta California (San Francisco), Aug. 8, 1858, p. 1.

BLOODY AFFRAY ON THE STANISLAUS RIVER

A correspondent of the *Stockton Argus* writing from Knight's Ferry under date of the 5th inst., gives the following account of the affray at Central Ferry on the 4th:

The difficulty occurred between some miners owning mining claims on "Grand Bar" and two Frenchmen owning shares in a claim opposite at the lower end of the bar. I was near the place at the time of the difficulty, but did not see it. I saw two of the men after they were shot. The particulars as I will give them to you, I obtained from one of the party who was standing by during the shooting: It appears that the company working the river claim had by means of a drain, raised the water so as to interfere with the working of the bar claim. Wednesday morning, about 5 o'clock, five of the miners owning bar claims went down unarmed for the purpose of trying to effect some arrangements with the river company. On arriving there, they found two Frenchmen (who were partners in the claim) at work wheeling dirt on the dam, and another of the owners standing on the bar. Some words passed between the parties which were unsatisfactory, when one of the bar miners took hold of the plank on which the Frenchman was wheeling and threw it off the dam. The smallest of the two Frenchmen then attacked the miner, while the larger one ran to his cabin and brought out two double-barreled guns and commenced firing at the party, the other Frenchman in the meantime, being free, ran up to the cabin, took the gun which had been discharged, reloaded it, and fired both barrels at the party, instantly killing one man and dangerously wounding another.

The gun appears to have been loaded with heavy buckshot. There were six shots fired in all. One of the wounded men received a portion of two charges in his body and is in a very critical condition. Another of the wounded men received three balls in his legs, and another, some distance from the place, was grazed in the side by a shot. The name of the man killed was Leonard Shoccob. The one dangerously wounded, Abram Lelay. George Crooks has three balls in his legs. After the shooting, the Frenchmen took their guns, pistols, ammunition and knives, started across the river and up over the hills, in the direction of Stockton. As the attacked party were without arms, and three of the five required assistance, they could not, of course, follow.

The *Stockton Republican* says: After the men were shot, a party of miners headed by Mr. Jacob Pike, who kept a store at Peoria, started in pursuit of the Frenchmen, three of whom were involved in the killing. One of the three had been a soldier, and is said to be a deadly shot at sixty paces. The fugitives were pursued over the Stanislaus into Tuolumne County, to Short Crop Bar, (two miles) and from thence up to Chapparal Mountain, which is in the same county. Here the pursued turned and commenced firing on the pursuers. Mr. Pike was instantly killed at the first fire, and Mr. Chas. McKenney mortally wounded. The Frenchmen continued their flight, and were last seen at the Mountain Saw Mill, two and a half miles from Sonora. The alarm was given in every direction, and Mr. Robert McMullen, Marshal of Columbia, Mr. Carden, and three other gentlemen, were promptly on the trail. A party also started from Sonora after the desperate fugitives. It is said that they cannot escape. Peoria Bar is some forty or fifty miles from this city [Stockton]. The Frenchmen had some twenty Chinamen employed on their work. Those remaining are much alarmed, as great excitement prevails. Mr. Pike has a brother in this city, one in Montezuma, and one a teamster on the road. He was about twenty-six years of age. The man first killed was a German.

Sacramento Daily Union, Aug. 19, 1858, p. 4.

THE STANISLAUS TRAGEDY

We publish from the Sonora correspondence of the *Bulletin*, under date of August 14th, what appears to be a correct version of the late shooting affair on the Stanislaus:

As no correct statement of these bloody murders has yet appeared in any of the published accounts, I propose briefly to give you the facts, which are as follows:

About one year ago, the French Company, some five in number, came on the river and "jumped" the claim about which this difficulty occurred. This claim belonged to Benjamin Lawhead. Crooks & Co. had a claim above — not on the bed of the river, but on "Grand Bar." Crooks & Co. had worked their claim for four years, during all of which time they held peaceable possession, and there was none who disputed their rights. About one year since, the French Company informed Crooks & Co. that they desired to turn the river below them and wished to know if it would interfere with their (Crooks & Co.'s) works. Crooks & Co. replied that it was impossible for them (the French) to work the claim below, for if they did so, they (Crooks & Co.) would have to stop operations, in consequence of the back water. The French agreed that they would construct their works so as to *lower* the water one foot. To this proposition Crooks & Co. assented. Accordingly, last season the French Company commenced operations; but, instead of lowering the water one foot, they *raised it seven feet*, and compelled Crooks & Co. to hire extra help in consequence thereof.

In November 1857, the river rose and drove all the miners from their work. Crooks & Co. then informed the French company that their dam (which was constructed of planks), was injuring them, and requested its removal. With this request the French company complied in part, by removing a portion of the dam. In July last, Crooks & Co. wanted to work the bottom of their claim, which was fifteen feet deeper than the bed of the river, and consequently removed the balance of the dam and let off the back water. The Frenchmen, after obtaining legal advice on the subject, found it necessary to lay their claim over until such time as it was workable. A portion of the French company, however, (the brothers Bigard), being not satisfied, the balance of the company sold out.

The brothers Bigard again commenced operations, and backed the water up on Crooks & Co. On the evening previous to the difficulty, Crooks went to the Frenchmen, and told them that it was impossible for both companies to work, that one company must cease operations. The Bigards replied that Crooks & Co. should come down next day, and they would have a consultation, and if they (the French) could not work without injuring Crook & Co., they would suspend operations till some other time. On the evening, I saw Webber, one of the French company, who told me that a portion of their company were in favor of compromising the matter, but for his part he was not willing to do so.

The next morning, 4th August, according to Agreement, Crooks & Co. went down to see what arrangements could be made. They found one man wheeling dirt, raising the dam. This man was the larger brother of the Frenchmen. Crooks told him to stop wheeling dirt, as it was backing the water into their hole in which they were working. The Frenchman stopped, went down to one of his partners (Webber), and after speaking to him, commenced wheeling again. While the Frenchmen was absent for a load of dirt, Crooks removed one of the planks upon which he was running the wheelbarrow. The Frenchman was not within twenty feet at the time, and of course was not thrown in the river, as is alleged by E. Valette. The large Frenchman then made for Crooks, who seeing that he was in great danger from so powerful an assailant, ran to the river and picked up a stone. When the Frenchman seized Crooks, the latter struck him with a stone. Crooks being a small man, the Frenchman threw him in the river. Crooks, however, retained his grip and took the Frenchman with him. Here the Frenchman attempted to drown Crooks, but he, being somewhat quicker in his movements, succeeded in disengaging himself from the iron grasp of his assailant, and sprang upon the dam. At this time, the Frenchman sung out to his brother (who had taken his position near a brush shanty close by), to "shoot." The brother immediately fired two shots, wounding two men and killing one. One of the wounded has since died. The man who shot then returned into the cabin and brought out another shot gun and fired one barrel. The other having failed to fire, he pricked some powder into the tube, put on a fresh cap, and took deliberate aim and tried to shoot, but the gun again refused to do the murderous work. By this time the first gun was reloaded, and while Crooks & Co. (those of them at least who were able), were retreating, and had got off some sixty yards, the large Frenchman fired both barrels, shooting Crooks for the third time.

The Frenchmen then armed themselves, each with a double-barreled shot gun, pistol and bowie knife, and traveled across the river into Calaveras county. In a short time, a number of miners went in pursuit, taking different directions. The murderers took to the mountains, and kept the ridge or high ground, so as to distinctly observe the movements of their pursuers, while the latter could not perceive them. One of the pursuing parties went up the river as far as Calaway's dam, and there re-crossed to the Tuolumne side of the river, thinking they would give up the chase for the present. It afterwards appeared that the Frenchman had crossed at the same place, and were but a short distance ahead, and had taken up their position in an elbow of the trail, where they could without difficulty shoot down all their pursuers. With their guns ready cocked, they stood until the foremost came within a few feet, when they opened their murderous fire, shooting Charles McKenny in the head, (which felled him to the ground.) Rodger McKue was shot in the breast, and Robert Warren received five balls in his side, penetrating the heart.

The killed and wounded now are as follows: Killed—Leonard Shock, Abraham Delevan, and Robert Warren. Wounded Geo. J. Crooks, Chas. McKenny, and Rodger McKue. The French were armed to the teeth, while the Crooks party were entirely unarmed.

This matter has created great excitement throughout the Southern mines, and it is due to the public to give the facts as they occurred. The E. Vallette who fathers the communication in the *Echo du Pacifique* is, in all probability, one Kegnier, who, I believe, reloaded the shot gun.

This is neither the *French* nor the *American* side of this unhappy story, but a plain statement of the facts as they occurred. Let the public make their own comments.

John F. Zollner,
of Peoria Bar, Stanislaus River.

CREDITS

Photographs

p. 27. A family photograph. [Jacob Pike and Drummers]
p. 30. A family photograph. [Jacob Pike]
p. 31. A family photograph. [Mary Pike]
p. 36. A family photograph. [Jacob Pike]

Maps

p. 9.   Created by Ben Pease, Pease Press, San Francisco.
p. 21. Created by Ben Pease, Pease Press, San Francisco.

ABOUT THE EDITOR

PETER PIKE JR. is a fourth-generation Californian who grew up in Marin County and attended the University of California, Berkeley. He served in the Peace Corps in Honduras (1965–67) and sailed across the Atlantic singlehanded (1972–1973). His book *California Bound: A Family Memoir* tracks Jacob Pike and three generations of ancestors in the Golden State from the 1850s to the 1940s. Retired from a business career in San Francisco, Peter lives with his wife, Dyan, in Greenbrae, California, and enjoys visits with their four grandsons.

Email: pikepeter1@gmail.com

www.ingramcontent.com/pod-product-compliance
Lightning Source LLC
Chambersburg PA
CBHW031127080526
44587CB00011B/1142